BELFAST
CITY HALL

One Hundred Years

In memory
of
Martin Lynn

BELFAST CITY HALL

One Hundred Years

Gillian McIntosh

BLACKSTAFF
PRESS

BELFAST
CITY COUNCIL

Contents

Foreword

Reading this book fills me with an enormous sense of pride: a pride not only in the splendour of the City Hall, but in the role this magnificent building has played, and continues to play, in the lives of the people of Belfast.

In 1899 the *Belfast News Letter* had proclaimed that 'we Belfast people are proud of our city and its many activities. We are in the very front of the race of civic development'. It was this spirit that the city fathers set out to capture in their plans for the City Hall, which was opened in August 1906 as a symbol of Belfast's enterprise and success, and a gesture of its faith in the future.

The centenary of the opening of the City Hall presents Belfast City Council with a unique opportunity to confirm its status as the impetus behind the development of the city. A modern example of the continuing ambition, confidence and foresight of the Council was the decision to build the Waterfront Hall. Opened in 1997, this project represented an investment equivalent in today's terms with that required to complete the City Hall. A catalyst for the regeneration of what in Victorian times was a highly industrialised area, the Waterfront Hall was voted runner-up in the World's Best Congress Centre AIPC APEX Awards of 2002. Belfast City Council continues to seek to place Belfast at the front of the race of civic development.

The architect who designed City Hall, Brumwell Thomas, described it as 'a monument to the character of the people of Belfast'. I would also wish to reaffirm to the citizens of Belfast that the City Hall is their building. This book will be distributed to every school in the city, and forms part of a range of centenary-year initiatives designed to reach out to all the people of Belfast.

I hope that you will enjoy reading this book and learning about the history of this wonderful icon of our city, the City Hall.

CLLR WALLACE BROWNE
LORD MAYOR

'From insignificance to vast importance'

In the twenty years that marked the last decade of the Victorian era and the reign of Edward VII, Belfast was a vibrant and flourishing city. 'No city in Ireland (if indeed any in the United Kingdom) has so rapidly developed itself from insignificance to vast importance as Belfast,' boasted the *Belfast and Ulster Directory* in 1897. Two years later, in September 1899, the *Belfast News Letter*, the voice of unionism, boldly declared: 'We Belfast people are proud of our city and its many activities. We are in the very front of the race of civic development … and we have a laudable ambition to keep there.' It was the spirit of the age that the city fathers, the architect and the builders set out to capture when they undertook the planning and construction of the new City Hall in Belfast, which opened its doors to an admiring public on 1 August 1906.

The ultimate expression of a pride and self-confidence rooted in the burgeoning city's commercial and industrial success, the construction of Belfast City Hall was begun in 1898 and completed in 1906.

The decision to build a new city hall was part of the broader improvement of Belfast that began in the 1860s and continued apace for the next half century, and encompassed public health, street improvements and sanitation. Thus, in typical Victorian style, the construction of the City Hall was motivated by both functional and symbolic needs. Civic buildings traditionally serve a number of functions, the minimum being to accommodate a town clerk's office, a treasurer's office and a council chamber, and most contain a large hall for public meetings and entertainments.

Almost from the moment it opened, the City Hall, Belfast's premier example of monumental public architecture, became the main venue for its citizens.

NATIONAL LIBRARY OF IRELAND

As with all monuments, the City Hall has come to represent many things to many people over the past one hundred years. But above all, it represents the genius loci of Belfast. In the early years it was a symbol of Victorian Belfast's enterprise and success and a gesture of its faith in the future, flowering in the Edwardian era to represent the stability of that period before the fracture of the First World War.

A stage for the social and political dramas of Ulster (and Ireland) in microcosm, Belfast City Hall became a popular venue within days of its opening, when the Apprentice Boys of Derry arranged to rally there ahead of their grand parade, while in July 1907 Belfast workers involved in the Dock Strike converged on the City Hall.

Over the years it has been the focus for domestic political campaigns, from the 1912 signing of the Solemn League and Covenant in opposition to Home Rule, to the 1985 protest rally against the signing of the Anglo-Irish Agreement. It has acted as the forum for civic demonstrations of celebration and protestation – from the ecstatic receptions for Mary Peters after her pentathlon gold medal win at the 1972 Munich Olympics and Barry McGuigan returning from his world featherweight title victory in the summer of 1985, to the large demonstrations against the war in Iraq and the peace rallies against local violence, sectarianism and racism at the turn of the twenty-first century.

In a period of turmoil few can forget the triumphal scenes that greeted Mary Peters when she returned to Belfast in 1972 with her Olympic gold medal.

GETTY IMAGES

Belfast welcomes Barry McGuigan after his world featherweight title victory in June 1985.

PACEMAKER PRESS INTERNATIONAL

For many the City Hall is synonymous with its enormous Christmas tree and the lighting of the city's festive lights.

SCENIC IRELAND

"GOLD PLATE" CIGARETTES 10 FOR 3ᴰ

GALLAHER Lᵗᵈ

NEW CITY HALL.

Gallaher, the tobacco manufacturers, was quick to spot the advertising potential of associating their cigarettes with the impressive new building.

BELFAST TELEGRAPH

The new building quickly became a trademark for Belfast, Gallaher, the tobacco manufacturers, using it as an image in their advertising campaign for Gold Plate cigarettes two days after it opened.

It became the principal subject in Belfast guide-books produced in the decades after its opening, providing their authors with a landmark building about which to wax lyrical and a visually impressive architectural expression with which to fill their pages. Today, for citizens and visitors alike, Belfast City Hall maintains the traditions of its origins. It is the city's venue for civic celebration on a private and a public scale, from weddings to the millennium festivities. It acts as host to countless numbers of guests from throughout the island, Great Britain, and indeed the world.

Throughout the century, Belfast City Hall has provided the city centre with spacious gardens in which to relax and meet friends.

SCENIC IRELAND

The *Builder*, in an article on town halls in 1878, commented
that 'possessing wealth is the prelude to architectural display'.
By the 1880s Belfast's modest Town Hall in Victoria Street
was no longer large enough to meet the needs of the city's
municipal government, either practically or symbolically.

BELFAST CITY HALL.

The Work has been under the control of Mr. JAMES G. GAMBLE, Clerk of the Works.

LIST OF CONTRACTORS.

Building Contract	Messrs. H. & J. MARTIN, Ltd., Belfast.
Heating and Ventilation	,, ASHWELL & NESBITT, Ltd., London.
Marble Work	,, FARMER & BRINDLEY, London.
Constructional Steelwork	,, CLYDE STRUCTURAL IRON CO.
Do. Do.	,, P. & W. M'LELLAN, Glasgow.
Stained Glass	,, WARD & PARTNERS, Belfast.
Do.	,, CAMPBELL BROTHERS, Belfast.
Plaster Work	,, GEORGE ROME & Co., Glasgow.
Modelling	,, THE BROMSGROVE GUILD, Worcester.
Electrical Work	,, WILLIAM COATES & SONS, Belfast.
Hydrants	,, WILLIAM COATES & SONS, Belfast.
Lifts	,, WILLIAM COATES & SONS, Belfast.
Do.	,, THE MEDWAY LIFT Co., London.
Carving	,, PURDY & MILLARD, Belfast.
Do.	,, H. H. MARTYN & Co., Ltd., Cheltenham.
Do.	Mr. J. E. WINTER, Belfast.
Plumbing and Sanitary Work	,, JOHN DOWLING, Belfast.
Electric Fittings	Messrs. J. W. SINGER & SONS, Frome.
Wrought Ironwork	,, FRANCIS RITCHIE & SONS, Belfast.
Clocks	,, GIBSON & Co., Belfast.
Strong Room Doors	,, MILNER & SONS, London.
Hot Water Service	,, MUSGRAVE & Co., Belfast.
Mosaic Pavings	,, DIESPEKER, Ltd., London.
Wood Block Flooring	,, ELLIS, GEARY & Co., London.
Safes	,, THOMAS SKIDMORE & SONS, Wolverhampton.
Locks, etc.	,, JAMES GIBBONS, Wolverhampton.
Carpets, Blinds, etc.	,, GILLESPIE & WOODSIDE, Belfast.

The Furniture was provided by Messrs. H. & J. MARTIN, Ltd., Belfast; GOODALL, LAMBE & HEIGHWAY, Ltd., Manchester; MAGUIRE & EDWARDS, Belfast; HAMPTON & SONS, London, and PARTRIDGE & COOPER, London.

39

The City Hall bears testament to the skill of the workmen who were employed on the project, and reflects the diversity of their origins from Glasgow to London to Belfast. This list of contractors is from W. & G. Baird's 1906 publication marking the opening of the City Hall.

A New Municipal Home for Belfast

The 1830s and 1840s were decades of municipal reform. There had been a Belfast Corporation since 1613, when the town received its charter from James I. The Corporation was reformed in 1840 and met for the first time in 1842, occupying a building in Victoria Square. The decade of the 1860s was one of expansion for the town, with, for example, the building of a municipal abattoir in 1869. As part of this growth, and as an articulation of civic pride, a new town hall was completed in Victoria Street in 1871 at a cost of £16,000. However, this, too, quickly became inadequate for the requirements of a rapidly growing town, which boasted 21,989 voters in 1881 and was finally granted city status in 1888. The expansion of Belfast was further evidenced in the 1890s, with Queen Victoria conferring the title of lord mayor on the city's mayoral office in 1892, and the extension of the city's boundary in 1896, resulting in an increase of wards from five to fifteen. Given the extension of their powers and responsibilities since 1842, the Belfast municipal fathers now felt that a new civic focal point was required, and aspired to a grander building.

The construction of the new City Hall was also part of a rebranding of Belfast, designed to beautify and glorify an industrial centre and impress the observer with its municipal civility. A monument to the Corporation, as well as to the city's industry and enterprise, the building also bears testament to the skill of Belfast workmanship.

In the final decade of the nineteenth century Belfast's political masters were determined to counter the dominant image of the city as one rife with religious division and disturbances. In 1800 Catholics had made up 6 per cent of the town's population, rising to 34 per cent by the end of the century. Tensions between the two religious communities were exacerbated by an influx of rural migrants, and sectarianism and rioting became a regular feature of the city's life. So prevalent was this perception of Belfast as a place of violence, it was reported

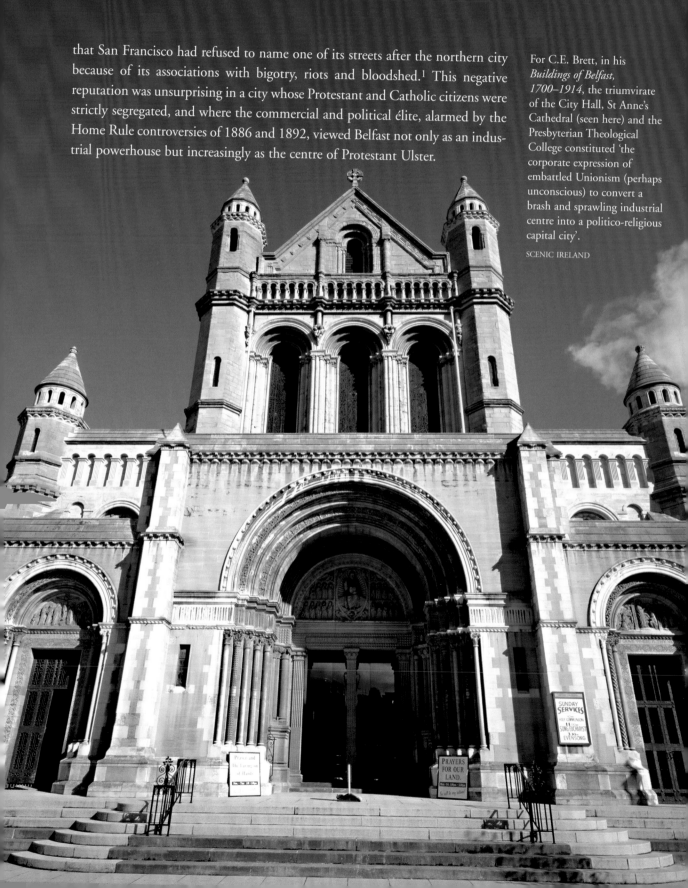

that San Francisco had refused to name one of its streets after the northern city because of its associations with bigotry, riots and bloodshed.[1] This negative reputation was unsurprising in a city whose Protestant and Catholic citizens were strictly segregated, and where the commercial and political élite, alarmed by the Home Rule controversies of 1886 and 1892, viewed Belfast not only as an industrial powerhouse but increasingly as the centre of Protestant Ulster.

For C.E. Brett, in his *Buildings of Belfast, 1700–1914*, the triumvirate of the City Hall, St Anne's Cathedral (seen here) and the Presbyterian Theological College constituted 'the corporate expression of embattled Unionism (perhaps unconscious) to convert a brash and sprawling industrial centre into a politico-religious capital city'.

SCENIC IRELAND

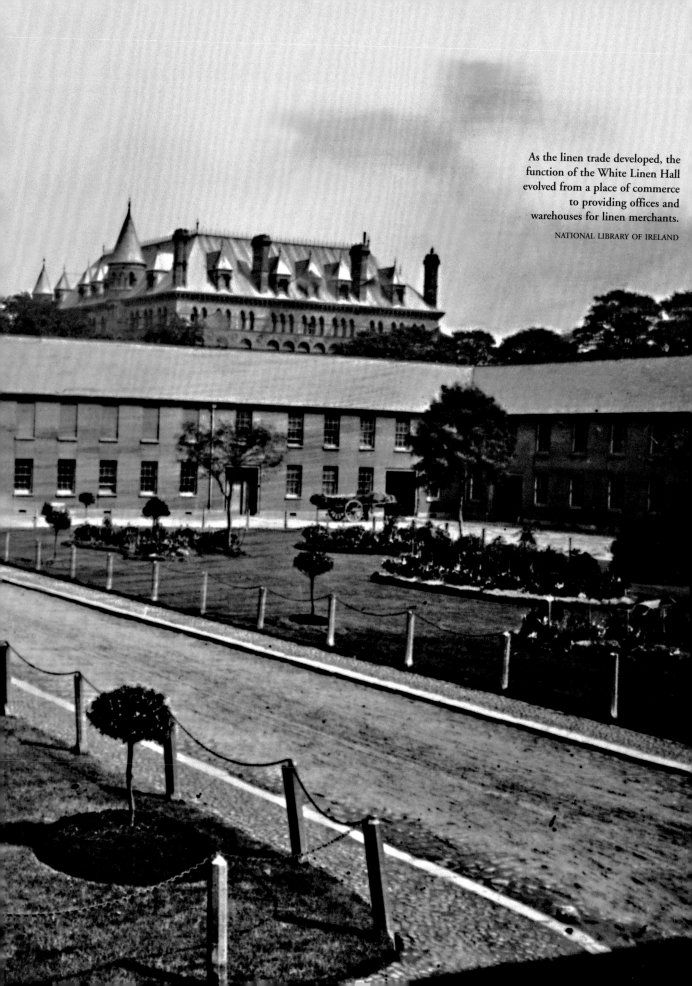

As the linen trade developed, the function of the White Linen Hall evolved from a place of commerce to providing offices and warehouses for linen merchants.

 ## The White Linen Hall

A suitable site for the new municipal centre soon became available. The countess of Shaftesbury had inherited the site of the White Linen Hall, which had dominated Donegall Square since the mid-1780s, and in 1888 indicated that she intended to sell the property. Erected at a cost of £10,000 in 1784, on a site granted in perpetuity by Lord Donegall, the White Linen Hall was funded by public subscription, with linen trading beginning there in 1785. A place for Belfast's middle class to promenade, it also provided a home for the Belfast Library and Society for Promoting Knowledge, which continues today as the Linen Hall Library on Donegall Square North.

Councillor C. Connor, a representative of the Committee of the White Linen Hall and a member of Belfast City Corporation, was the first to advocate the purchase of the site for the new City Hall. A meeting was convened on 15 November 1888 between Connor, Lord Mayor James Haslett, the solicitors acting for the White Linen Hall and the countess of Shaftesbury to discuss how to proceed. Initially, the countess had intended that the buildings of the White Linen Hall should be removed from the site, and the 'whole space thus made available laid out as a public garden'.[2] This was characteristic of a general Victorian desire for public parks, evidenced in 1869 when Belfast Corporation bought the abandoned Donegall demesne at Ormeau and made it into the town's first public park. Ormeau was followed by others, including Alexandra Park in 1885, Woodvale in 1888, Dunville and Victoria in 1891 and Botanic Gardens (in existence since the 1820s but not in

Linen Hall Library
SCENIC IRELAND

public hands) in 1894. However, the more pressing concern for the Corporation was the increasingly cramped conditions of the Town Hall in Victoria Street, which meant that some town officials had to be housed outside the building. Arguably, they were also motivated by the desire for a landmark building with which to reflect and enhance their own status and that of their city. The countess was eventually persuaded that the site could in part be used to erect a city hall, with the rest of the grounds laid out as public gardens.

Paying for the City Hall

A bill to authorise the proposed transfer of the site and to provide for the distribution of the purchase money was given royal assent on 25 July 1890, and the buildings of the White Linen Hall were eventually removed six years later in February 1896. Four Acts were passed to provide the funding for the new building. The first, passed in 1890, authorised £30,000 for the site and £180,000 for the construction of the building. In 1899 a second Act granted another £30,000; a third in 1902 granted £50,000 'for the completion of the city hall and buildings and the fitting and furnishing thereof'; and in 1905 a final Provisional Order amending the Belfast Act 1902 granted Belfast Corporation an additional £40,000 to complete the building and for the 'improvement and enclosing of the grounds adjacent to and used in connexion with the city hall'.[3]

An invoice from the architect, Brumwell Thomas, due to Messrs Farmer & Brindley, London, for marble work in the City Hall, 1905

Local Government Board Inquiries

Both the Belfast Act 1902 and its amendment in 1905 resulted in Local Government Board inquiries into the cost of the City Hall. In the course of the 1905 inquiry the Local Government Board inspector, on being told that the foundation stone had cost £500, wondered sarcastically if it was made of a

For nearly a century the White Linen Hall dominated Donegall Square.

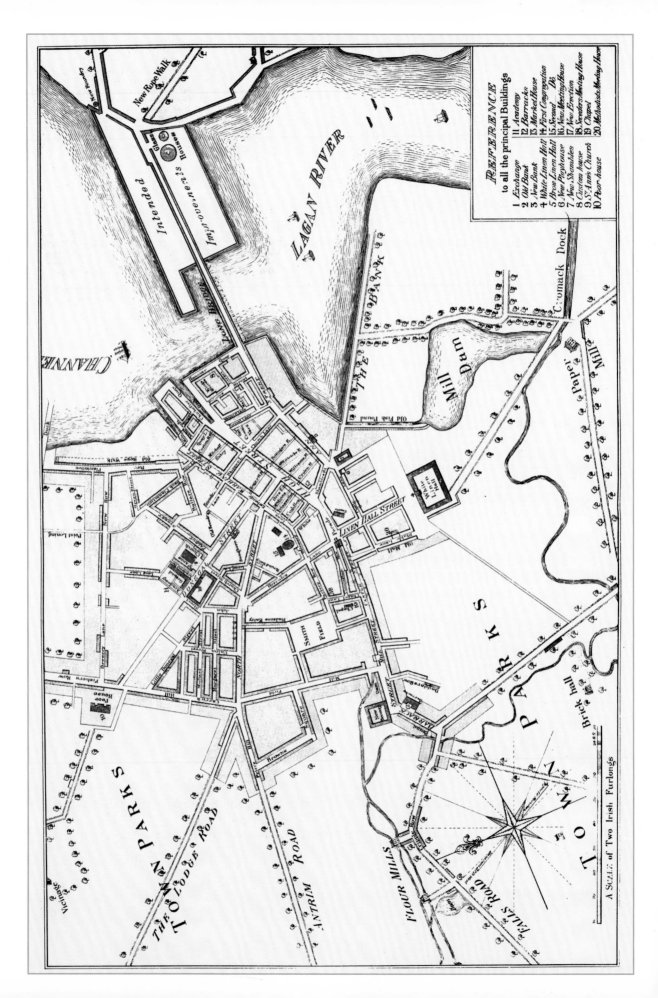

precious stone. A harassed town clerk, Sir Samuel Black, clarified that the money included the cost of the ceremony for the laying of the foundation stone.

Funded in part from the profits of the municipal gas industry, the City Hall eventually cost over £360,000 to complete. In today's terms, using the index of average earnings, that is equivalent to £128 million. Moreover, in the spring of 1907 the architect, Alfred Brumwell Thomas (1868–1948), issued a writ for almost £14,000 for the balance of his fees. The builders H. & J. Martin also threatened to sue the Corporation for an outstanding balance of £67,000, but before litigation (and after a private conversation with the lord mayor) the company agreed to settle for £33,000.

The runaway cost of the City Hall was due to a combination of factors: an unrealistic idea of what such an undertaking would entail in terms of expenditure; an insistence on the use of only the finest raw materials; and the hiring of mostly Corporation labourers and local contractors, who were relatively more expensive than their counterparts in Great Britain. In evidence to the 1905 inquiry, Councillor William McCartney, chairman of the improvement committee, gave his explanation of the cost:

> This building was started by an old and dying Corporation in 1897, a month before the enlarged Corporation came in. It was increased then to sixty members.

Donegall Place in 1903 decorated for the royal visit of Edward VII and Queen Alexandra

BELFAST TELEGRAPH

OPPOSITE:

The municipal move from Victoria Street altered the entire orientation of Belfast, from the quays and the River Lagan to Donegall Square.

LINEN HALL LIBRARY

During the Local Government Board Inquiry conducted in 1905 into the cost of the City Hall, Sir Samuel Black, the town clerk, reported that the Belfast construction company H. & J. Martin had been asked by the Corporation to erect hoarding around the building site. This proved to be necessary because the Corporation had received complaints that the building work was frightening horses and injuring the public. Giving evidence to the inquiry, Councillor J.J. McDonnell, JP, reported that H. & J. Martin was renting the hoarding as advertising space to the Belfast Advertising Company for the sum of £5,000.

MAGNI

The whole personnel of the committees was changed, and it was like beginning a new thing over again.

As the project developed, the exponential rise in expenditure was also due in great part to the enthusiasm of Belfast's councillors, who, excited by the possibilities of the building, were willing to approve various changes to realise their aspirations for their new municipal home. At the inquiry, counsel for the Corporation accepted this explanation. According to A.K. Overend: 'Any increase in expenditure on the Town Hall has been due entirely to the increased ideas of the Council from time to time.' Thus, even before work had begun on the City Hall, its proposed height was raised, which consequently altered the plans for staircases and flooring. Asked at the inquiry when the question of economy had ceased to be considered, Brumwell Thomas replied, 'The moment the first variation was made to the building … I began to see that once you raised the building by putting an additional five feet in it, there would be no end to the changes that would follow.'

The extension of the public hall on the east of the building had knock-on effects; a gallery costing £3,000 (equivalent today to £1 million) was added at an advanced stage in the construction. And the plasterwork, originally planned to be simple and allocated a budget of £2,100, was considered too plain when viewed by the members of the Corporation. They subsequently gave the architect permission to commission more elaborate plasterwork, which they felt would be in keeping with the grander tone of the building, adding a further £5,000 to the cost.

P.C. Cowan, the Local Government Board inspector, was particularly critical of the manner in which the Corporation had managed the budget for the construction of the City Hall. He felt that the architect should have been asked for costings more frequently. Costly delays may also have been exacerbated by Thomas's commitment to another major project. In 1906, the same year that Belfast City Hall was opened, he completed another municipal building – the more modest Woolwich Town Hall.

Despite the two inquiries into its cost – a full-page celebration of the building in the *Belfast Telegraph* on the day of its opening declaring in a large strapline, 'Total cost over £300,000' – the price ultimately became a point of local pride.

The scale and grandeur of the City Hall was a bold statement and its cost did not deter the architectural ambitions of Belfast's political élite, many of whom were involved, fifteen years later, in the decision to build another impressive building that also went greatly over budget – Parliament Buildings, Stormont.

The elaborate plasterwork replaced the previously plainer plasterwork at a total cost of over £7,000.

BELFAST CITY COUNCIL

From Town Hall to City Hall

The Gas Department refused to use electricity in its offices in the City Hall. This despite the Corporation's pride in the city's new electricity station, opened on the day the City Hall's foundation stone was laid. The insistence on retaining gas in one part of the building also added to the spiralling construction costs.

GETTY IMAGES

The decision to move from Victoria Street and invest in the site in Donegall Square had not been an easy one. While the Corporation had agreed to the erection of a city hall in November 1894 (by a vote of 21 to 15) and reaffirmed its commitment in January 1895, it was not until November of that year that the resolution to build was passed. A month later a sub-committee was established to decide on the requirements of the building.[4] It was this committee which agreed that, in addition to a large central hall and a tower, the new building should have a porte-cochère, reflecting the Greek influence so prominent in Victorian architecture. When the building was revealed in 1906, however, this was the feature most criticised by architectural observers.[5]

The later 1870s had seen the improvement of the street geography of a large part of the city centre, in particular the laying out of a grand new thoroughfare between Donegall Place and York Street, which swept away the old butchers' quarter of Hercules Street and its warren of alleys and entries. Royal Avenue was subsequently completed in the 1880s. During this regeneration of the city streetscape, initial Corporation debates about the City Hall concentrated on its orientation in Donegall Square. Councillor William McCormack suggested that it face Donegall Square West, with its back to Donegall Square East, thus allowing Donegall Place to continue on to Linenhall Street.[6] But the current position of the building, fronting Donegall Square North and with a vista down Donegall Place, a premier address for Belfast's upper middle class in the nineteenth century, won the day. For Thomas, however, as he recalled forty years later in the *Belfast News Letter* on 1 August 1946, in the early days of the project the building's orientation was not his major concern but, rather, whether the ground would bear the weight of the structure, particularly the dome. With no precedent to guide him, he trusted that it would, and it did.

Eventually, the specifications for the new building, drawn up by the City Surveyor J.C. Bretland, were sent to the Council of the Royal Institute of British Architects, and in June 1896 the RIBA was asked to recommend three architects for 'the guidance of the Corporation' when appointing an assessor. In the second half of the nineteenth century there was only one person for the job – Alfred Waterhouse (1830–1905).

A distinguished architect in his own right, famous for the Natural History Museum in London and Manchester Town Hall, Waterhouse was noted for a professional approach rather than any brilliance or innovation in his own design work. His large institutional buildings favoured the Gothic style. In his role as architectural adjudicator, he influenced the selection of the design of many of the major public buildings of the later nineteenth century, and in the case of Belfast City Hall he was assisted as assessor by Bretland.

The competition for the new City Hall was advertised in the *Irish Builder* in June 1896. The cost of the building was not to exceed £125,000. The journal anticipated that many architects would apply for this prestigious commission

This architect's drawing from the *Irish Builder* of 1 January 1900 shows the entrance porch to the public hall on the east side of the City Hall.

The City Hall from Donegall Place, *c.* 1910

RIGHT: The influence of classical and Renaissance architecture on Brumwell Thomas is most apparent in the use of marble throughout the interior and the dominance of the Ionic columns.

NATIONAL LIBRARY OF IRELAND

Alfred Waterhouse (1830–1905) was appointed architectural assessor and paid £300 for his expert opinion.

NATIONAL PORTRAIT GALLERY

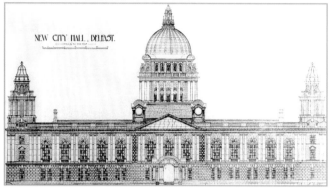

PRONI

and, in the end, fifty-one plans were submitted. The *Irish Builder* of this period also reveals the improvement and advancement of Belfast's middle and upper classes, who were moving from the city centre to the new suburbs of Malone and Sydenham. The journal's pages advertise designs for the new villas that would grace the expanding suburbs of the city.

By March 1897 Waterhouse had chosen the plans of E. Thomas & Son, Westminster, the name of 28-year-old Brumwell Thomas's company. Three runners-up – Graeme Brett (Belfast), Malcolm Starks (Glasgow) and Roantree (Glasgow) – were awarded a prize of £100 each. Thomas's design reflected the concerns of Victorian architects, who looked for inspiration to classical and Renaissance architecture.

Architect of the Natural History Museum in London (left) and Manchester Town Hall (below), it was as an architectural adjudicator that Alfred Waterhouse had most significant influence; in the period 1864–99 he assessed at least sixty competitions, of which Belfast City Hall was one.

NATURAL HISTORY MUSEUM, LONDON, AND MANCHESTER CITY COUNCIL

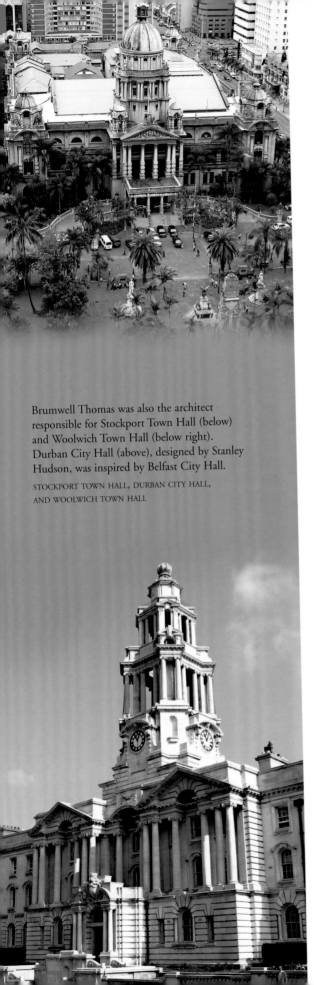

Brumwell Thomas was also the architect responsible for Stockport Town Hall (below) and Woolwich Town Hall (below right). Durban City Hall (above), designed by Stanley Hudson, was inspired by Belfast City Hall.

STOCKPORT TOWN HALL, DURBAN CITY HALL, AND WOOLWICH TOWN HALL

Sir Alfred Brumwell Thomas was born in 1868 at Virginia Water in Surrey. After training at Westminster Art School, he ran his own practice from 1896, with an address in Piccadilly. He was made a fellow of the Royal Institute of British Architects in 1906 and knighted the same year. He died on 22 January 1948. He was one of the most successful exponents of the Baroque revival, which became the fashion for public buildings of the early 1900s. His principal works are the town halls of Stockport (1905), Woolwich (1906) and Belfast (1906). He also designed the Dunkirk and Belfast war memorials.

The Architect

Belfast City Hall was not only a testament to its age and its backers, but remains an enduring monument to Brumwell Thomas, who was knighted on its opening. The architect, commented the *Belfast News Letter* in August 1906, designed the City Hall as 'a monument to the character of the people of Belfast … a monument of the time in which it was reared'. This was Thomas's first success in competition for a large building, and it led to other similar (albeit less grandiose) commissions. He designed Stockport Town Hall (inspired by Belfast City Hall but at a cost of under £57,000) and Woolwich Town Hall. Unquestionably, Belfast City Hall is his crowning glory, and his work in Belfast began a life-long attachment to the city, to which he remained a frequent visitor until his death in 1948.

With the architect in place, tenders for the erection of the building were publicly advertised (with the Schedule of Quantities and Form of Tender available from the architect or surveyors for a five-guinea deposit). W.H. Stephens was selected as quantity surveyor, and the prominent Belfast building firm H. & J. Martin was awarded the contract in October 1897.

The Surveyors and the Builders

The company W.H. Stephens began life as S. & W.H. Stephens, brothers from Kilkenny who opened surveyors offices in both Dublin and Belfast in the mid-nineteenth century. Over the next century and a half (in 1900 becoming simply W.H. Stephens) they were the surveyors who oversaw much of the building of an improving Belfast. Similarly, H. & J. Martin was a very successful company with an impressive list of contracts and commissions throughout Ireland, constructing, for example, the North Wall and South Wall in Dublin Harbour and Penrose Quay in Cork. Indeed, one son managed a branch of the firm in Dublin. In Belfast alone, as the *Belfast Evening Telegraph* reported on 18 October 1898, the company was responsible for the engineering works at Albert Quay and part of Donegall Quay, the sewerage drains for the majority of the city, the diversion of the Blackstaff river, the Free Public Library in Royal Avenue, the new offices of the Harbour Commissioners, Robinson and Cleaver's department store, the Grand Opera House and the new offices of the Water Commissioners. Further afield, the firm built the new pier and promenade in Bangor and the Slieve Donard Hotel in Newcastle.

At the time of the construction of the City Hall, H. & J. Martin was also involved in the

The City Hall's builders were also responsible for the new offices of the Harbour Commissioners.

MAGNI

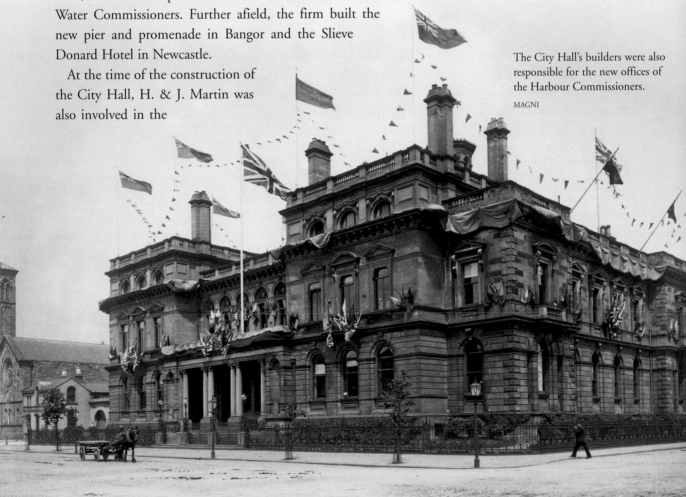

Belfast City Hall under
construction, May 1903

MAGNI

A.R.HOGG. 28. MAY. 1903.

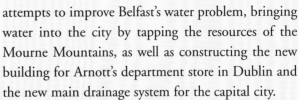

attempts to improve Belfast's water problem, bringing water into the city by tapping the resources of the Mourne Mountains, as well as constructing the new building for Arnott's department store in Dublin and the new main drainage system for the capital city.

Belfast City Hall was a reflection of the city's Victorian self-confidence and provincial pride, built on the wider commercial success of Ulster. The generated wealth, of course, was not evenly shared among its citizens and large numbers of people continued to live in impoverished and unsanitary conditions. Yet, as historian W.A. Maguire comments, this was Belfast's heyday. And in a rapidly expanding and changing city, with a population that had doubled from 175,000 to 350,000 between 1871 and 1901, the City Hall was indeed an expression of the bold independence and individuality that were such features of Belfast politics in the early twentieth century. In a period of political and social change the new building was, simultaneously, a statement of self-confidence and certainty, as well as a declaration of intent, with Belfast's city fathers looking for security in stone. It was also a time in which the structure of urban government was completed, with the municipalisation of gas, electricity and public transport.

Changing the City's Landscape

For the residents in the neighbourhood of Donegall Square and Donegall Place there was a rapid change in their urban landscape – in 1899 the building to house the Ocean Accident and Guarantee Corporation was begun in Donegall Square East, in 1902 the Scottish Provident Building was completed in Donegall Square West, in 1906 the new City Hall was officially unveiled, and in 1907 the Municipal College of Technology, equipped with all the latest technological and scientific facilities, was opened in nearby College Square East. In this vein, the City

Hall also embodied technological advancement. For example, in 1897 the Corporation insisted that instead of traditional chimneys and fireplaces, a new way of heating the City Hall be found. And in order to minimise its discolouration by soot, the exterior of the building was washed with a special solution to ensure an 'agreeable tint in weathering'.[7]

The buildings of Donegall Square enhanced the general effect of the City Hall 'by the charm of contrast or of comparison', one observer noted.[8] As C.E. Brett has argued, these 'very large and grandiose building ventures were required to express a new sense of self-importance'. For historian Cornelius O'Leary, the ambition of Belfast City Hall articulated a desire to compete and outdo the great English cities, rivalling 'any British civic temple' in scale and magnificence.

Laying the Foundation Stone

A ceremonial trowel and a gavel were presented to Lord Cadogan, the lord lieutenant of Ireland, to mark the laying of the foundation stone in October 1898.

BELFAST CITY COUNCIL

Ireland's lord lieutenant, Lord Cadogan, came to lay the foundation stone for the new City Hall on 18 October 1898. He was met at the Belfast and County Down railway station at Queen's Quay by Sir James Henderson, the lord mayor, and members of the Corporation (who had generously voted themselves new robes to celebrate the occasion) and a guard of honour drawn from the Liverpool Regiment, reported the *Irish News*. Escorted by the Inniskilling Dragoons, the party arrived at the Donegall Square site, where they were met by a large crowd and a guard of honour drawn from the Staffordshire Regiment, who also provided a guard of honour at a later reception in the Ulster Hall in Bedford Street.

During the ceremony, a time capsule was placed in a large glass bottle under the foundation stone, containing coins, local newspapers, a copy of the Belfast Corporation diary for 1898, a description of the future City Hall and the new electricity station, a souvenir medal, and a phonographic recording of Sir James Henderson, William Pirrie, a former lord mayor and member of the sub-committee which had decided on the requirements of the building, and Sir Samuel Black, the town clerk. In his address to the lord lieutenant, Black drew attention to the growth of the city and to those industries crucial to its success – shipbuilding and linen. He linked the foundation-stone ceremony with the new electricity station on East Bridge Street, which the lord lieutenant would open later that day, the two events reinforcing the message of Belfast's modernity. Setting his remarks in an all-Ireland context, with Belfast established as the model for others to aspire to, he expressed the hope that 'self-reliance and steady industry will be the rule and not the exception over the length and breadth of the land'. Brumwell Thomas presented Lord Cadogan with a ceremonial trowel and John Martin, of H. & J. Martin, presented him with a ceremonial gavel.

Duties completed, the ceremonial party joined four hundred invited guests for luncheon at the Ulster Hall. During the speeches of welcome, Henderson formally announced the Corporation's intention to erect a statue of Queen Victoria in front of the City Hall. Lord Cadogan, in reply, dwelt on a contemporary debate about the question of Catholic universities and, according to the *Irish News* report, spoiled the luncheon with 'cold-blooded insinuations … regarding Northern intolerance and bigotry'. Although praising Belfast for its 'growth, wealth and prosperity' and its self-reliance, the key themes associated with the new building, the lord lieutenant asked that those of the majority population in Ulster opposed to a Catholic university should look on it from a patriotic point of view and with more tolerance. Barbing his compliments, he concluded his speech with the wish that Belfast would act as a model to others as it became one of the leading cities of the world. Alluding to its riotous reputation, he also hoped that as the city grew, accumulating wealth and influence, it would also set an example as peaceful and law abiding.

The City Hall represented not only the ambition and self-confidence of the Victorian age but also the short-lived self-belief and apparent stability that marked the Edwardian age. The building opened in 1906 in a changed economic climate from that in which it had been under construction. The 1890s had been boom building years in Belfast and came at the end of a period of municipal construction. During this time of civic building, the Queen's Bridge (1843), the Courthouse (1850), Custom House (1857), Water Office (1869) and Town Hall (1871) were all constructed. In the period 1901–14

The new electricity station was opened on East Bridge Street on the day the City Hall's foundation stone was laid, linking the two buildings and drawing attention to Belfast's modernity.

MAGNI

CITY OF OTTAWA

National War Memorial, Ottawa

RIGHT: The memorial to the men of the Royal Irish Rifles who were wounded, killed in action, or died of disease in the Boer War is by Sydney March (1876–1968). An accomplished sculptor, March was responsible for busts of Edward VII and Cecil Rhodes, as well as the National War Memorial in Ottawa, which he created with members of his family. The Boer War sculpture was unveiled in October 1905 by Lord Grenfell, commander-in-chief in Ireland, and was the first of many war memorials housed in the City Hall. The monument was moved to the east side of the building in 1926 during the creation of the Garden of Remembrance and the erection of the Cenotaph.

NATIONAL LIBRARY OF IRELAND

that rapid building phase came to an end. Additionally, the shipbuilding industry, celebrated in the statue of Sir Edward Harland in the grounds of the City Hall, entered a difficult period after the end of the boom in merchant shipping created by the Boer War. The industry recovered gradually, thanks mainly to the business acumen of William Pirrie, and led to the launch of the *Olympic* in 1910, and its sister ship *Titanic* in 1911.

By 1914 the output of the two Belfast shipyards, Harland & Wolff and Workman Clark, was one-eighth of the world's production. With steady improvements in its harbour, Belfast was, in the early decades of the twentieth century, a great port. On the eve of the First World War the city was also the biggest producer of rope and linen in the world. In *The Truth about Ulster*, published in 1914, F. Frankfort Moore wrote:

> Belfast is really a wonder. It can launch the largest ships that the world has ever seen; it can spend nearly a quarter of a million making a dock that will enable the biggest ships in the world to be repaired; it has the largest rope works in existence, and the largest spinning mill. For the production of such luxuries as whiskey and tobacco in marketable form Belfast stands pre-eminent in the Customs list. For a variety of industries, and for every one of them all being a world's record in production, there is no city in the kingdom that can compete with Belfast.

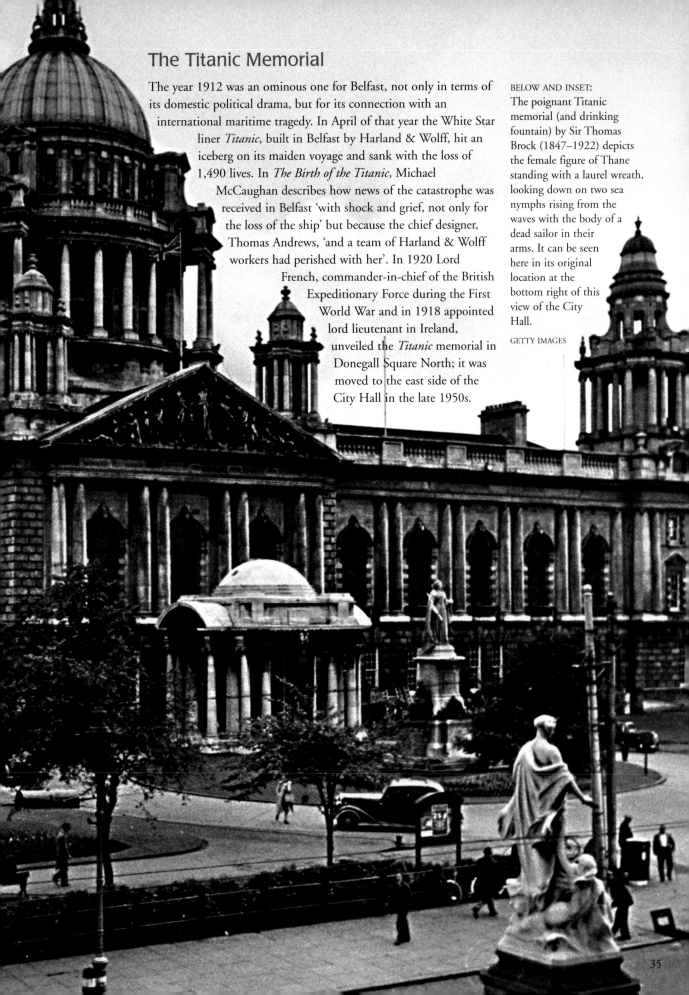

The Titanic Memorial

The year 1912 was an ominous one for Belfast, not only in terms of its domestic political drama, but for its connection with an international maritime tragedy. In April of that year the White Star liner *Titanic*, built in Belfast by Harland & Wolff, hit an iceberg on its maiden voyage and sank with the loss of 1,490 lives. In *The Birth of the Titanic*, Michael McCaughan describes how news of the catastrophe was received in Belfast 'with shock and grief, not only for the loss of the ship' but because the chief designer, Thomas Andrews, 'and a team of Harland & Wolff workers had perished with her'. In 1920 Lord French, commander-in-chief of the British Expeditionary Force during the First World War and in 1918 appointed lord lieutenant in Ireland, unveiled the *Titanic* memorial in Donegall Square North; it was moved to the east side of the City Hall in the late 1950s.

BELOW AND INSET:
The poignant Titanic memorial (and drinking fountain) by Sir Thomas Brock (1847–1922) depicts the female figure of Thane standing with a laurel wreath, looking down on two sea nymphs rising from the waves with the body of a dead sailor in their arms. It can be seen here in its original location at the bottom right of this view of the City Hall.

GETTY IMAGES

The Dufferin and Ava Monument

The west side of the City Hall features a memorial to the first marquess of Dufferin, who had been governor-general of Canada (1872–8), British ambassador to Russia (1879–81) and to Turkey (1881), viceroy of India (1884–8), and British ambassador to Rome (1888) and to Paris (1892). The most famous member of the Blackwood family of Clandeboye, County Down, Frederick Hamilton-Temple-Blackwood thus had had a distinguished diplomatic careeer. This monument, unveiled by the marquess of Londonderry on 9 June 1906 and costing £5,000, was principally the work of Frederick Pomeroy (1856–1924), who invited Alfred Brumwell Thomas to collaborate with him on the monument in 1903. Thomas's contribution is the stone base and canopy, designed in Italian Renaissance style to complement the City Hall, and from which rises the figure of Fame.

The Dufferin statue is offset by a turbaned Indian astride a cannon and holding a sabre, and a snowshoed Canadian with musket, sitting on a dead moose, and is enshrined in a small temple that bears a remarkable resemblance to the City Hall itself. Pomeroy trained as an architectural carver and was involved in the Arts and Crafts movement. As that movement declined, he focused more on commissions for portrait busts and monuments to politicians and churchmen, but remaining true to his training, he always believed in the need for a sculptor's work to be bound up with that of the architect. One of his most significant pieces is the Curzon memorial (1912–15), which stands in Calcutta. The Dufferin and Ava monument was moved to the edge of the Garden of Remembrance in the 1920s.

NATIONAL LIBRARY OF IRELAND, MAGNI AND
SCENIC IRELAND

Supplement to "NOMAD'S WEEKLY." Saturday, May 26, 1906.

WANTED
A MAN TO OPEN
THIS BUILDING
ONE CONNECTED WITH
ROYALTY, OR ABLE TO
MAKE A FEW MORE
KNIGHTS PREFERRED.
NO REASONABLE APPLICATION
REFUSED.
APPLY TO ME. Dan

Sir Dan: "Ma gawd, I didn't think it would come to this."

This *Nomad's Weekly* cartoon features Sir Daniel Dixon, lord mayor when the building opened, but who had admitted to the Local Government Board Inquiry in 1905 that he had originally been against the building of the new City Hall altogether. It was, according to Dixon, William Pirrie, lord mayor 1896–7, who had had the 'big ideas' in relation to the City Hall; unsurprising, perhaps, given Pirrie's own personal wealth and extravagance.

LINEN HALL LIBRARY

The Grand Opening

The City Hall was opened in a baptism of wind and rain on 1 August 1906. The weather accented the gravity of the day, commented the *Irish Builder* on 11 August 1906, with the reflection that the people of Belfast were 'a persistent people, clear of purpose, strengthened by strenuous climate, quickening their step to brightness when it comes, but nowise moved from their path by gloom'. There was no great pageantry to mark the day, no great effusiveness but, rather, interest and 'a decorous pride', according to the journal. Although the Corporation had hoped that Edward VII would perform the ceremony, the honour fell to Lord Aberdeen, the lord lieutenant.

Accompanied by Imperial Yeomanry, Lord and Lady Aberdeen approached the City Hall from Donegall Place and were presented the royal salute by the Royal Inniskilling Fusiliers. At the porte-cochère they were met by the lord mayor, Sir Daniel Dixon, and the aldermen and councillors of the city, who presented Aberdeen with a gold key, bearing, in enamel, the city arms, the lord lieutenant's arms and a view of the City Hall, made by the Belfast firm Gibson & Co. In the entrance hall, Brumwell Thomas, John Martin and William McCartney, given pride of place, were presented to Lord Aberdeen. In his speech, Lord Aberdeen praised the building and touched on the impressive development of technical education in Belfast (the Municipal College of Technology opened the following year) and expressed the hope that the housing situation would improve. Described by the *Irish Builder* as 'distinct as to sound, but almost incoherent as to meaning', his speech was mercifully a short one for the two thousand guests attending the ceremony.

In his speech at the opening of the City Hall in August 1906, reported by the *Belfast Telegraph* on 2 August 1906, Lord Aberdeen, the lord lieutenant, saw in the fabric of the new building a reflection of Belfast and its citizens:

The massiveness of this noble structure typifies the sure and stable foundations of the prosperity and welfare of this great city and community; may the beauty and grace of the design and execution of this building and its artistic features symbolise, and more than symbolise, the culture of all that is best in public and private life, the promotion of all that is true and lovely and of good report: and above all, may the benediction of the Almighty be sought and obtained for all the transactions, for all the high purposes, which shall be dealt with in this centre of a great city.

While a large number of guests filled the Council Chamber, the remainder were housed in other rooms in the City Hall; and in the Great Hall an ode, specially written for the occasion by Lisburn poet Samuel K. Cowan, was performed to music composed by Dr Koeller:

> 'Arise! Advance!'
> And we have risen, and advanced, and never
> Thro' change or chance,
> Swerved from the path of earnest endeavour!
>
> A little town
> Hath grown a mighty city, thro' the thrift
> That stamps Wrong down,
> And thro' those thews of Truth, that never drift
> From Creed and Crown!

At the luncheon in the Banqueting Hall, which followed the morning's ceremonies, both Lord Aberdeen and Brumwell Thomas paid particular tributes to Ward and Partners (Belfast), the firm responsible for the design and execution of the majority of the glasswork throughout the building. Indeed, their contract for the glasswork was the 'largest public order for stained glass paid for by public capital in Ireland ever given to an Irish firm'. For Thomas, Ward and Partners' work had two things to commend it – it was excellent and it was local, something of which the people of Belfast could be proud. Campbell Bros of Franklin Street, Belfast, executed the glasswork on the dome and towers.

The *Nomad Weekly*'s less reverent comment on the opening of the City Hall contrasts sharply with the generally glowing praise of other press coverage.

LINEN HALL LIBRARY

THE MUNICIPAL GILT CAGE OPEN.

ABERDEEN: "Blessed if I don't think it would have been cheaper to the ratepayers to have wrung your neck. However, now that I have opened the door, go inside and have more sense."

ABOVE:
The sumptuous Great Hall, which was rebuilt after almost total destruction by a German air raid in May 1941.

LEFT:
The Great Hall as it was when first rebuilt.

BELFAST CITY COUNCIL

41

The new City Hall was an instant draw for
the public, and was portrayed in countless
photographs and postcards. The Belfast
photographer Alexander Robert Hogg
(1870–1939) is seen here lying beneath the
dome of Belfast City Hall, photographing it
for the commemorative book which was
issued by W. & G. Baird in 1906.

MAGNI

CAPRICORNVS

The architect similarly commended the excellent wood carving carried out by Purdy & Millard and J. Edgar Winter (both Belfast firms) and by H.H. Martyn and Co. of Cheltenham.

In addition to the local trades involved in the project (William Coates & Sons of Belfast was responsible for the electrical work, for example), many firms from Britain were also employed. The marble work, mosaic paving, and wood-block flooring were all the handiwork of London tradespeople. Glasgow provided the structural steelwork and plasterwork, while Manchester supplied some of the furniture for the new building. Historian Asa Briggs has commented that the riches of Victorian England were lavished on the new town hall in Leeds in the mid-nineteenth century. One could argue the same for Belfast City Hall. Thomas also paid warm and special tribute to the clerk of works James Gamble, who supervised the project, given that the architect was largely based in London. Gamble, who had also been the clerk of works for the city's new abattoir and electricity station, reported his typical working week to the Corporation in 1898:

I have often [correspondence] to do after working hours, when as a rule, I am in very bad form, and, with the worry and constant standing on my feet, I am sometimes very tired … I come here [to the City Hall site] as a rule at 6 o'clock am, and last week was engaged up to 9 o'clock for two nights, and to 8.15, 8.30, and 8 o'clock for the three other evenings, making an average day of over 14 hours (of course less meals).

For his labours, Gamble was paid four and a half guineas a week.

OPPOSITE:
At a height of 173 feet, the dome of the City Hall is a familiar Belfast landmark.

BELFAST CITY COUNCIL

The City Hall's Statues

During his speech at the opening of the City Hall, Lord Aberdeen drew attention to the statues already present in the grounds and expressed the hope that they would inspire the 'best aspirations of the youth of the city'. Just as the building itself encapsulates Victorian Belfast, the statues commemorate those Victorians who had made the city what it was in this period.

Statues in the City Hall grounds today

SIR EDWARD HARLAND

Sir Thomas Brock's statue of Sir Edward Harland, head of Harland & Wolff and lord mayor of Belfast in 1885–6, was paid for by subscription from a fund of nearly £1,000 and unveiled by the earl of Glasgow, president of the Institute of Naval Architects. Brock's career took off when his father-in-law, John Henry Foley, died suddenly and he had to take over his commissions, the most famous of which is the 42-foot-high monument to Daniel O'Connell which dominates O'Connell Street in Dublin. By the 1890s, Brock led the field in official sculpture. Responsible for the new coinage head of Queen Victoria in 1891, no other living sculptor had produced more portraits of the queen. The unveiling of Harland's statue, the first to be erected in the grounds, took place in June 1903 during a visit of the Institute of Naval Architects to Belfast.

BELFAST TELEGRAPH

NATIONAL LIBRARY OF IRELAND

SIR JAMES HASLETT

Frederick Pomeroy's sculpture of Sir James Haslett, druggist, prominent Orangeman, lord mayor in 1887–8, Conservative MP for West Belfast in 1883 and 1886 and North Belfast in 1896 and 1903, was unveiled by the marquess of Londonderry in April 1909. Wearing the lord mayor's chain of office, Haslett (known as Oily Jemmy because he had made his fortune in the importation of paraffin oil) is represented standing in an oratorical position, with his hand resting on a small table, on which lies the mayoral robe. The statue was designed to harmonise with that of Sir Edward Harland.

ENIC IRELAND

DERMOTT DUNBAR

SIR DANIEL DIXON

Sir Daniel Dixon, lord mayor in 1892–3, 1901–3 and 1905–6, as well as chief magistrate and chairman of the Harbour Board, by Sir William Hamo Thorneycroft (1850–1925) was unveiled by the earl of Shaftesbury in August 1910. Like many of Belfast's lord mayors, Dixon was a man of some means. On 28 July 1906 the *Northern Whig* reported that Dixon had paid for the entertainment on the occasion of the opening of the City Hall, and that over the term of his mayoralty he had paid a total of £20,000 for municipal entertaining. Thorneycroft was noted for the powerful realism of his work, a key component of the New Sculpture movement. He was a protégé of Alfred Waterhouse, the City Hall competition's assessor.

ROBERT McMORDIE

Robert McMordie, lord mayor 1910–1914, became a member of Belfast Corporation in 1907, representing Victoria Ward. He was MP for East Belfast from 1911 until his death on 25 March 1914. Despite this relatively brief civic career his wife Julia McMordie was in a position to ensure he was not forgotten. She herself had an impressive civic record. She was made an Hon. Burgess in 1914, was elected a member of Belfast Corporation in 1917, became an alderman of Belfast in 1920 and was MP for South Belfast in the Northern Ireland parliament from 1921–25. She was awarded an OBE in 1919, the year her late husband's statue was unveiled.

DERMOTT DUNBAR

BELFAST CITY HALL CENTENARY

Edward VII and Queen Alexandra enter the grounds of
the City Hall during their visit to Belfast in 1903 to
unveil the statue of Queen Victoria.

MAGNI

In 1900 the new building was showing above ground level, and by 28 July 1903 work had progressed sufficiently to allow Edward VII and Queen Alexandra, on their Irish tour, to unveil Sir Thomas Brock's statue of Queen Victoria. The royal presence in Belfast was greeted generally with great enthusiasm, with bunting and cheering crowds. In his 1946 interview in the *Belfast News Letter*, Thomas recalled that the ceremony of the unveiling provided a 'pleasant interlude in the midst of the building work'.

In his speech, reported in the *Illustrated London News* on 1 August 1903, the king commented on the manufacturing enterprise of Ulster and to his 'pride in the position that Belfast had won among the cities of the Empire'. His speech was therefore reflective of all the concerns of Belfast's élite in terms of the city's image, and all they hoped the new City Hall would represent. After the ceremony, Edward VII also found time to open new extensions to the Royal Victoria Hospital, before lunching in the Town Hall in Victoria Street.

Interestingly, the statue of Queen Victoria was not the first to be unveiled in the grounds. Perhaps hinting at the dominance of the local over the imperial, that honour went to the statue of Sir Edward Harland, of the shipbuilders Harland & Wolff and former lord mayor, also by Sir Thomas Brock and unveiled in June 1903. Given that it was due to men such as Harland that Belfast had progressed so rapidly, necessitating the extravagant new City Hall, this seems appropriate. Symbolically, the statue was erected on the east side of the City Hall, towards Queen's Island, where Harland's large shipyard was located. In a reception following the unveiling, reported in the *Belfast Telegraph* on 25 June 1903, William Pirrie, speaking to over two hundred guests in his home at Ormiston (such soirees were not uncommon at the Pirrie residence), boasted of Belfast's world place in shipbuilding and engineering. In the statue of Harland, he said, they were reminded of the enterprise and progress that were a feature of the late shipbuilder and, by association, a feature of Belfast. It was an honour, he declared, that both Harland and the shipbuilding industry were recognised with a memorial in such a central location.

The statue of Queen Victoria is the most dominant in the grounds of the City Hall. Criticism was laid against its location in front of the much maligned porte-cochère, thus blocking the entrance to the building. In the words of the *Irish Builder* in 1905:

All are giving each other guesses as to the nature of the erection in front of the centre. Some guess it to be a porte-cochère, but these are jokers … The majority incline to consider it a mausoleum for the statue of Queen Victoria which, she not liking, stepped out of, with her pedestal, to the open ground.

NATIONAL LIBRARY OF
IRELAND

During their visit to Belfast
in July 1903, Edward VII and
Queen Alexandra unveiled
Sir Thomas Brock's statue of
Queen Victoria.

MAGNI

ILLLUSTRATED LONDON NEWS

In the central role it was to play many times over the century, in June 1921 the City Hall acted as the impressive backdrop to the civic reception for the royal visit on the occasion of the inauguration of the Northern Ireland parliament.

The grounds of the City Hall thus became a place where Belfast's mercantile élite could be honoured, their significance to the fortunes of the city recognised and reinforced by the grandees who unveiled their monuments. In this way, in April 1909, Sir James Haslett, the lord mayor who had negotiated the purchase of the White Linen Hall site in 1888 and who died in 1905, was memorialised in a statue by Frederick Pomeroy.

Haslett was followed by another crucial figure in the history of the City Hall – Sir Daniel Dixon, property developer and three times lord mayor, during whose mayoralty the building had largely come into being and who died within a year of it opening. Robert McMordie, solicitor, Conservative MP for East Belfast and lord mayor during the politically turbulent years of 1910–14, was the last of the men who were significant to Belfast and to the City Hall to be so honoured. His statue, also by Frederick Pomeroy and unveiled by the dowager marchioness of Dufferin and Ava in May 1919, drew to a close the period of memorialising the individual in the grounds of the City Hall. All the statues honoured their subjects and, by extension, the city they had helped to create and the municipal palace they had helped to build. The City Hall, in turn, reinforced their status and that of their city.

The Splendour of the Building

The splendour of the building was celebrated in a commemorative book, written by Alfred Brumwell Thomas and published by local publishers W. & G. Baird in 1906, and available at half a crown. But for all the praise heaped on the City Hall, there were critical voices as well, complaining about the extravagance of the building.

In typical Victorian character, Belfast City Hall was functional as well as symbolic, providing accommodation on the ground floor for the Town Clerk's Department, the City Surveyor's Department and the City Cashier's Department; on the first floor, the departments of the City Accountant, the Medical Officer and the Electrical Engineer, as well as the Gas Department; the second floor housed the departments of Education, Works, Markets, and Weights and Measures. However, it was as a symbol of mercantile success and Victorian self-confidence that the City Hall spoke loudest, as evidenced by the way in which it was filled with paintings of local notables, many produced by prominent Victorian artists such as Henrietta Rae.

Built in classical Renaissance style, the building was faced with 30,000 tons of Portland stone, supplied by the Bath Stone Firm. It is rectangular and encloses a quadrangular courtyard. Facing Donegall Place, its two-storey façade is 300 feet

Sir James Haslett's statue was moved from its original position in 1926 when the grounds of the City Hall were being rearranged.

MAGNI

long. The second storey is the more attractive, with large arched windows and Ionic columns arranged in pairs between each window. On the upper storey, eight columns support a triangular pediment, the most dominant feature of the façade, which celebrates in relief the city's mercantile heritage. The tympanum of the pediment contains an allegorical group, sculpted by Frederick Pomeroy and J. Edgar Winter at a cost of £2,000. The central figure represents Erin, with Minerva (goddess of wisdom) and Mercury (god of trade, profit, merchants and travellers) in attendance and taking under their protection shipbuilding and navigation. On Erin's left, Fama (goddess of fame and rumour) awards the palm (the symbol of victory, distinction and rejoicing) to a worker bearing a finished web of linen, while a spinner at her wheel represents another branch of the textile industry. The tympanum thus articulates the industries that had contributed to Belfast's growth and success.

The Victorians were enormously influenced by the visual, and Belfast City Hall is nothing if not visually impressive. Dominating the entire building is the central dome, supported by a drum of masonry encircled by a colonnade of Ionic pillars and crowned by a stone lantern. At 173 feet, it is the building's most imposing and identifiable feature.

Nevertheless, for the *Irish Builder*, reporting on 11 August 1906, an overriding defect was that building did not have a sufficient base, which would have given the structure more height. Moreover, the journal frowned on the two porches, particularly the porte-cochère, and its report went on to argue that the statue of Queen Victoria had been placed too centrally and too close to the building. It should rather have been set to one side and balanced on the other by a statue of Edward VII.

Belfast citizens viewing their new City Hall. Later, on the fortieth anniversary of the opening of the building, the *Belfast News Letter* boasted that Belfast was a 'capital city' and that its City Hall 'was a symbol of its fame and prestige, as well as an expression of its spiritual and cultural ideals'.

Brumwell Thomas's drawing of the portico on the City Hall's east side.

BELFAST CITY HALL CENTENARY

The City Hall's dome is described
by C.E. Brett, in his *Buildings of
Belfast, 1700–1914*, as 'a light-buoy
marking out the centre of Belfast'.

SCENIC IRELAND

The Grand Staircase of Carrara, Pavonazzo and Brecia marbles, the work of Farmer and Brindley of London, has a domed ceiling. On the principal landing, the same marble is repeated, with the addition of some Greek Cippalino marble. For Thomas, the 'greatest moment' of all came on the day when 'the City Council authorised the scheme of marble decoration in the entrance hall and grand staircase'. Forty years later, he told the *Belfast News Letter* that while he hesitated to remember what it all cost, he still believed that it was the 'making of the building'.

The extensive use of marble and stained glass adds drama to the City Hall's interior.

BELFAST CITY COUNCIL

The main entrance and the Grand Staircase.

Red brick in the suburbs, white horse on the wall,
Eyetalian marbles in the City Hall:
O stranger from England, why stand so aghast?
May the Lord in His mercy be kind to Belfast.

from 'Ballad to a Traditional Refrain' by Maurice James Craig

'The most captious critic will confess that it is a noble hall of state, and worthy of the municipal palace of a great and flourishing city' – Robert Johnstone writing in his guide to Belfast in 1909

SCENIC IRELAND

The view from the Whispering Gallery, including John Luke's mural of Belfast receiving its town charter.

SCENIC IRELAND

Stained-glass Windows

The beautiful stained glass is a prominent feature throughout the City Hall.

In August 1900 the *Irish Builder* noted with pride that much of the work in the new building was being carried out by Belfast firms. Indeed, it dedicated a feature to the stained glass of the 'magnificent Municipal Buildings'. The original glasswork, carried out by Ward and Partners and Campbell Bros, followed the designs of Thomas. Throughout the building, the journal commented, the stained glass embodied in heraldry and picture 'the leading historical events and personages in the rise and progress of the city'. Thus, the Grand Staircase is flanked by seven stained-glass windows, illustrating the history of Belfast Corporation. Over the hall landing, three windows display the Belfast coat of arms, and portraits of Edward VII and Queen Alexandra. The windows record important dates in the history of Belfast, from the granting of the charter by James I in April 1613 to 1899 when the city was granted the status of a county borough. The East Staircase and Corridors are illuminated with seven windows, representing the royal arms. Of these, the largest window displays the royal arms and on both sides the shields of Belfast, Ulster and Ireland. The Banqueting Hall's stained-glass windows display the royal arms, the arms of Belfast and the arms of the city's founders, Lord Donegall and Lord Shaftesbury.

In the oak-panelled Reception Room, the three stained-glass windows represent the arms of the City, the royal arms of Edward VII and the arms of Lord Chichester. Above the Whispering Gallery is a ring of stained-glass windows displaying the signs of the zodiac, alternating with the ship and the bell taken from the quarters of the arms of the city.

This statue in bronze of Frederick Richard Chichester (1827–53), earl of Belfast, is by Patrick MacDowell (1799–1870), the Belfast-born sculptor responsible for a number of portrait statues, including William Pitt and the earl of Chatham for Westminster Palace, and *Europe*, one of the four great groups around the Albert Memorial in London.

Chichester's statue had originally stood in College Square East and was then housed in the Free Public Library before being moved to the City Hall.

In the Council Chamber the stained glass illustrates the arms of Lord Dufferin and Lord Londonderry, as well as the royal arms and the arms of Belfast. British monarchs who had visited Belfast – William III, Queen Victoria and Edward VII – are commemorated in three of the seven stained-glass windows in the Great Hall. The remaining four display the shields of the four provinces of Ireland.

The tradition of commemorating Belfast's history in glass has survived up to the present day. Commemorative windows to Belfast's Famine victims and to civilians and members of the Royal Ulster Constabulary killed since 1969 were unveiled in the City Hall in 1999, followed in 2005 by a window to those whose organs were removed in Northern Ireland hospitals without the knowledge of their families.

The famine window

BELFAST CITY COUNCIL

The ship image is taken from the arms of the city of Belfast.

Two stained-glass windows on the landing of the Grand Staircase commemorate Sir Crawford and Lady McCullagh. Sir Crawford McCullagh (1868–1948) dominated the position of lord mayor in the first half of the twentieth century. Knighted in 1915, he was lord mayor over three periods: 1914–16, 1931–42, and 1943–6. A former Unionist MP for South Belfast and a member of the Northern Ireland Senate, he was a director of Classic Cinemas, Maguire and Patterson, and a dry-goods business. His obituary in the *Belfast News Letter* gives a flavour of his career:

> During his business career he bought some valuable blocks of property in Castle Market and Castle Place, and in making these purchases he gave proof of his foresight and also of his faith in the growth and continued prosperity of Belfast. At one time he was the largest individual ratepayer in the city.

This goes some way to explaining how McCullagh could afford to be lord mayor for such an extended period, given that his lavish entertaining was funded from his own purse. The windows represent events from the McCullagh era, including the bombing of the City Hall on 5 May 1941.

THE COVENANT

Being convinced, firmly and deeply, that the use in porridge of inferior quality imported Oats would be disastrous to the physical well-being, health, happiness and, therefore, the prosperity of Ireland, our beloved country, not to mention the destruction it would bring on one of our oldest industries,

We, men and women of Ireland, subjects of His Most Gracious Majesty King George V., and without distinction as to creed or party, and putting the twin interests of our country and our health before all other considerations, and knowing that we hereby pledge ourselves not to accept, support, encourage, or in any way countenance any Oatmeal other than WHITE'S WAFER OATMEAL, the finest Oatmeal the world produces, made in Ireland from Irish Grown Oats (New Season's Crop) by Irish Labour. In furtherance of this, our solemn pledge, we promise to use all fair means that may be found necessary.

In sure confidence that we are right in our solemn resolve and decision as set forth above.

We hereto subscribe ourselves

THE MEN AND WOMEN OF ALL IRELAND.

Women signing the Ulster Women's Unionist Council Declaration on Ulster Day.
PRONI

The Solemn League and Covenant, 1912

With only a few years to rest on its laurels as an architectural marvel, the City Hall rapidly became the iconic space in Belfast. While St Anne's Cathedral represented the city's religious space for the majority, and the Custom House remained the space for political speeches and protest gatherings, the grounds of the City Hall became the space where citizens gathered to commemorate events of importance to civil society – such as war and peace.

In the early decades of the twentieth century two principal events altered the image of the City Hall irrevocably – the signing of the Solemn League and Covenant in September 1912 and the opening of the Northern Ireland parliament in June 1921. In particular, the signing of the Covenant, the most impressive domestic political display of resistance in Ulster, perhaps in the United Kingdom, in the twentieth century, marked the City Hall in a high-profile and partisan way as a symbol of unionist power and Protestant culture.

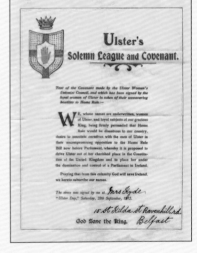

An enduring image of Ulster Day, 28 September 1912, is that of Edward Carson, with James Craig close at hand, signing the Solemn League and Covenant in the City Hall surrounded by the Unionist leaders.
PRONI

Custom House Square was the site associated with civic protest in Belfast for the first half of the twentieth century, and was famous for mass rallies during the Dockers' strike in the 1900s and the Outdoor Relief rallies of the 1930s.

NATIONAL LIBRARY OF IRELAND

Historian D. George Boyce has described the period before the third Home Rule crisis as one of those 'long, wary truces' in Irish history. Motivated by the desire to resist self-government for Ireland, Ulster unionism developed rapidly in the first decades of the twentieth century. The Ulster Unionist Council was created in 1905, Edward Carson was adopted as Unionist leader in 1910, and Unionist politics was militarised in the period 1911 to 1914, climaxing in the creation of the Ulster Volunteer Force in 1913.

The signing of the Solemn League and Covenant was the peak of a series of theatrical Unionist demonstrations articulating their opposition to the British government's plans for Home Rule for Ireland. The Covenant pledged its signatories to resist 'by any means that might be found necessary' the conspiracy against them. The concept of conspiracy was rooted in the belief that the formation of the Liberal government in 1911, achieved through an alliance with the Irish Parliamentary Party, and the subsequent removal of the House of Lord's veto that allowed for the introduction of the third Home Rule Bill, was an illegitimate use of a parliamentary majority. Moreover, the policy of Home Rule had not been an election issue in 1911, thus Ulster Unionists argued that it did not have the British public's mandate. In the end such arguments were lost in the tumult of the First World War, which caused the Act to be suspended for the duration of the hostilities. In the aftermath of the war the political landscape of Ireland was irrevocably changed, when new forces in the shape of Sinn Féin and new agendas in the form of demands for an Irish republic held sway.

Built on the site of the original Georgian church, St Anne's Cathedral became the religious centre for Protestant worship in Belfast.

SCENIC IRELAND

The signing of the Covenant was preceded by over a week of rallies throughout Ulster. Edward Carson and the Unionist hierarchy did the rounds of these rallies, whipping up popular support. Inspired by the Scottish covenants of the sixteenth and seventeenth centuries, and quasi-religious in nature and solemnity, the Solemn League and Covenant was also ratified by the Protestant Churches. The rallies climaxed with a spectacular demonstration in the Ulster Hall on 27 September, where Colonel R.H. Wallace, Provincial Grand Secretary of the Orange Institution, presented Edward Carson with a flag said to have been carried before William III's forces at the Battle of the Boyne.

The signing on the following day was very much a choreographed event. Mementos – from copies of the pledge to special fountain pens – were available to mark the occasion. On one level a day's entertainment, it was listed in the 'What's on today' columns of most Belfast newspapers. Details of the proceedings were advertised in the press days in advance, and the *Belfast News Letter* reported on 24 September that the Unionist Clubs of the city were organised to provide a 'guard of 2,500 men, divided into 5 reliefs of 500 each, to prevent injury to the City Hall gardens'.

Ulster Day marshals
gathered for prayers
in the City Hall
courtyard, prior to
the signing of the
Covenant.
PRONI

BELOW: Ulster Day
PRONI

An 'armed guard' (armed with broom handles) was placed on the City Hall from early in the morning, to protect the 'home of the Covenant', according to the *Irish News* on 30 September 1912.

PRONI

Following a religious service in the Ulster Hall, Unionist leaders marched to the City Hall to sign the Covenant.

GETTY IMAGES

Ulster Day and the signing of
the Covenant at the City Hall
became one of the iconic images
in the history of Ireland.

The signing of the Covenant was primarily a show of force, going beyond the mass demonstration of anti-Home Rule support in the 1892 Ulster Unionist Convention, and clearly showing Ulster unionism's military potential. The massive numbers who thronged Belfast, queuing in orderly lines to make their pledge, was an impressive sight.

The signing was preceded by a religious ceremony in the Ulster Hall, conducted jointly by the Church of Ireland and the Methodist and Presbyterian Churches, imbuing the event with a further air of respectability.

After the service, the leaders marched to the City Hall, where they were met, in front of Queen Victoria's statue, by Lord Mayor Robert McMordie and members of the Corporation in their civic robes, members of the Harbour Board, the Water Commissioners, and members of the Board of Guardians. Carson, Craig and the rest of the Unionist leaders then signed the pledge under the dome of the City Hall.

They were followed by the throngs outside the City Hall who were admitted in lots of five hundred to sign at specially constructed tables, entertained while they waited by bands playing loyal airs.

Signings were co-ordinated at centres throughout the province and ultimately the Covenant was signed by over 218,000 men, and a supplementary declaration of support was signed by over 234,000 women.[9]

Tables were specially constructed to accommodate the large number of men gathered at the City Hall to sign the Covenant.

MAGNI

The arresting backdrop and forum for the event was provided by the City Hall, the 'magnificently pillared and domed marble lined municipal palace', in the words of the *Northern Whig* report of the event, a far cry from the wooden pavilions of the 1892 Convention at Botanic Gardens. 'It was a wonderful sight that presented itself to the gaze of any spectator who could view the scene from the City Hall grounds,' reported the *Belfast News Letter* on 30 September 1912. 'Belfast was a city of Union Jacks,' the report continued, the Ulster Day Committee having made a special request to businesses and people to display the flag. The dramatic nature of the occasion was obvious in the descriptions of the scenes by the *Belfast News Letter*:

In the city itself people gazed with interest and approval on the illuminations at the

City Hall and the Ulster Hall. In front of the dome of the former building glowed the watchword of the province – 'We will not have Home Rule,' and those words were also illuminated over the entrance to the Ulster Hall, with the additional declaration – 'Ulster will Fight.'

The organisers thus set a precedent by transforming the building into a giant propaganda billboard, more than seven decades before the display of the 'Belfast Says No' banner on the City Hall in protest at the Anglo-Irish Agreement.

In contrast, for the nationalist *Irish News*, the partisan nature of the proceedings overarched all:

A crowning insult was paid to the city ratepayers who are non-Unionists – there are some left it appears even after Ulster Day – by the utilisation of the City Hall dome to blazon forth in illuminated capitals the worn-out war-cry of the local Tories.

In its biting report, the *Irish News* drew attention to the transformation of the building, which 'was formerly regarded as the headquarters of a supposedly non-political and impartial municipal administration'. Given that Sir James Henderson, Belfast's former lord mayor, had been on the organising committee for Ulster Day this was clearly not the case. The newspaper continued disdainfully:

The revolutionaries, the 'National Guard' of Belfast, distinguished by their tri-coloured armlets, stood around the City Hall grasping their besom shafts for the better part of three hours 'protecting' this edifice, now definitely recognised as the sacred temple of Toryism and Orangeism.

The signing of the Solemn League and Covenant imbued the City Hall with added meaning, elevating it from an expression of civic pride to one of domestic political drama. For the unionist *Belfast News Letter*, it transformed the City Hall

From early on Ulster Day crowds gathered outside the City Hall to sign the Solemn League and Covenant, see the leaders of Ulster unionism, and participate in the political drama of the day.
PRONI

More than two decades
after the signing of the
Covenant, the Albert
Clock was stopped and a
young man was paid to
strike the bell by hand as
Sir Edward Carson's
cortège passed through
the city in 1935.

MAGNI

from the centre of Belfast to the centre of Ulster loyalty. On the one hand, the nationalist *Irish News* declared that the City Hall was being used as a political playground, on the other, the *Belfast News Letter* argued that Belfast Corporation was not a political body and that permission to use the City Hall for the signing was 'another indication that Home Rule is not regarded as a question of ordinary party politics by the citizens and their representatives'.

As Edward Carson left Belfast at eleven o'clock that night, on the way to anti-Home Rule demonstrations in Liverpool and Glasgow, supporters were still

The statue of Edward Carson in the grounds of Parliament Buildings, Stormont.
SCENIC IRELAND

signing. His bodyguard at the dock was made up of members of the Queen's Island Unionist Club, who fired a volley of revolver shots as he boarded the steamship *Patriotic*. This was an indication of things to come. Although unarmed in September 1912, the unionist rank and file would not remain so for long. The announcement of the formation of the Ulster Volunteer Force (UVF) came in January 1913 and by September of that year the Ulster Unionist Council put in place a Provisional Government, whose proposed home was the City Hall.

Although the City Hall had played the most central and dramatic part in the signing of the Covenant, the old Town Hall also had a role in the 1912–14 Home Rule crisis. It was a signing venue for late Covenanters who had missed the Ulster Day event, and became the home of the UVF between 1913 and 1914. The Municipal College of Technology provided premises for the UVF's bakery. And despite the fact that all these places were supported by everyone's rates, both Catholic and Protestant, they were clearly regarded by Ulster Unionists as Protestant territory.

This period of unionist history is immortalised and celebrated in the reliefs around the plinth of the Carson statue, unveiled in front of Parliament Buildings, Stormont in 1933, which represent the signing of the Covenant, the rally in the Ulster Hall on its eve and Carson reviewing the UVF in 1913.

Significantly, when Edward Carson died in 1935, his funeral cortège stopped twice on its way through Belfast – at the old Town Hall in Victoria Street and in front of the City Hall.

Indeed, the Covenant continued to have cultural and political resonances throughout the twentieth century. On the occasion of the Covenant's jubilee in 1962, the Northern Ireland government, believing that the commemoration would provide 'unique opportunities' to publicise the state, declared its anniversary a public holiday and organised a commemorative demonstration and rally at Balmoral Show Grounds. This despite the clear disapproval of the British Home Office:

> While it is not a matter for us, we have felt some surprise, since the object of the Ulster Covenant was to resist, by illegal means if necessary, the proposals of the lawfully constituted government of the country, that it is proposed to give official sanction to these celebrations by declaring a Bank Holiday … the celebrations may presumably lead to some disorder; and we cannot exclude the possibility of critical comment by some sections of opinion in Great Britain.[10]

In November 1985, in a clear attempt to echo the success of Ulster Day, 1912, 200,000 people attended a massive rally at the City Hall to protest against the Anglo-Irish Agreement.

PACEMAKER PRESS INTERNATIONAL

The City Hall and the First World War

Within a decade of its opening, the City Hall became a monument to the First World War and Ulster's contribution to it. This was achieved with additions to the building in the form of commemorative tablets, statues and stained-glass windows.

The experience of the First World War, in particular that of the Battle of the Somme in July 1916, was to mark Ulster Protestant opinion and self-perception irrevocably. As war historian Keith Jeffery puts it: 'It marks the Union sealed with blood. It stands for the ultimate test of Ulster's loyalty; a blood-sacrifice to match any made by Irish Nationalists.'[11] The importance invested in the war had been evident from the beginning in the almost devotional reaction of unionists to the creation of the 36th (Ulster) Division in 1914, made up from the ranks of the UVF; its subsequent decimation at the Somme was profoundly traumatic and this is evident in its enduring place, to the present day, in unionist history, mythology and iconography.

War enthusiasm in Ireland generally mirrored that across Europe but, as elsewhere, it had particular local effects. In the south of Ireland it united unionists and nationalists in a joint war effort, with both groups volunteering for the same regiments. Unionist Ulster remained distant from the rest of the country, the desire for separateness particularly clear when they sought and were granted their own division. Lord Kitchener, the war minister, was persuaded that the UVF should form the nucleus of the 36th Division of the British army. The 36th was certainly unique, being overwhelmingly Protestant and unionist in nature. The mass enlistment of Ulster Volunteers created a division that accurately represented unionist Ulster. The makeshift uniforms of the UVF were replaced by the standard British army uniform, with tin hat and puttees. To this regular uniform, the division was granted permission to add the red hand badge of Ulster, a significant public concession to their separate identity by the British administration.

The 36th Division and the UVF were seamlessly forged into one in the minds of all, especially those in Ulster. As the *Belfast Evening Telegraph* reflected on 10 May 1915:

On 10 May 1915 the *Belfast Evening Telegraph* described the march past of the 36th (Ulster) Division at the City Hall: 'On, like a restless flood, four deep, tramp, tramp, tramp, past the saluting base, where every head turns like well-oiled machinery, down Chichester Street the long line goes. The sight sends the blood rioting through one's veins, and stirs the spirit like a trumpet call.'

MAGNI

Over all brooded a sense of solemnity, which was accentuated by the terrible disaster of the ocean [the *Lusitania* had just been sunk off the south coast of Ireland]. The spectators realised that these brave men were shortly going forth – many of them to find a grave in a foreign land, and others to endure wounds and suffering, but all to serve the Empire loyally, which is the key note of the UVF.

In the post-war period, and in the context of the armed rebellion of the Easter Rising in Dublin in 1916, when articulating pride in a paramilitary force that had threatened civil war in Ireland was problematic, unionists could thus express pride in the 36th Division.

36th (Ulster) Division

The 36th Division did not cross the Irish Sea to training grounds in Sussex until the summer of 1915, training instead in the intervening period in camps located across the province. This enhanced the new recruits' strong, and already well-established, identification with Ulster. In a display of pride, the division marched through Belfast on 8 May, the salute taken at the City Hall by General Sir Hugh McCalmont. The building imbued the occasion with solemnity, as the *Belfast Evening Telegraph* reported:

> Backed by the splendid outlines of the building itself, with its cupolas and dome, there is something dimly suggestive of the Imperial destiny of the British race about this aspect as presented from Donegall Place. It is some time, perhaps, before one realises that its most striking feature is the fine statue of Queen Victoria, which emerges with calm dignity from behind the forest of wood work, and its presence dominates the scene.

On the stand erected in front of the City Hall, Sir Crawford and Lady McCullagh, the lord mayor and lady mayoress, members of the Corporation and guests gathered to review the troops. In just over a year these same soldiers played a central role in what historian Paul Fussell has termed the most 'egregious, ironic action of the whole war' – the Battle of the Somme.[12]

Of the 100,000 British army recruits involved in the attack in July 1916, 60,000 were killed or wounded. The 36th Division suffered 5,000 casualties. Owing to war censorship, which became particularly stringent after the Somme (reflecting the extent of the carnage), little of the battle's human tragedy appeared in the press commentaries. It is in the lists of the war dead in the press that the impact of the Somme becomes apparent. The *Belfast News Letter*'s daily column, 'Ulster and the War', went from an average of two columns to five. The headlines in the press told their own story; for days after the battle they read, 'Ulster's Sacrifice' and 'Ulster's Sacrifice for Empire', and the losses at the Somme drew Ulster's unionist community together in grief. A resolution passed by the Corporation in the aftermath of the battle reflects its impact:

> The Citizens of Belfast reverently pay homage to the heroic dead. Young men in the prime of manhood who have laid down their lives and resigned the bright

hopes of youth and love, and ambition, to save their country from the fate of Belgium, Servia [*sic*] and Poland.[13]

Armistice Day, 1918

In November 1918, while the world was in the grip of a severe influenza epidemic, the First World War came to an end. In Belfast news of the armistice filtered slowly through the city and was enthusiastically received. As the evening progressed the *Irish News*, on 12 November 1918, reported incidences of 'rowdyism' from shipyard workers vandalising a cinema, and several 'mobs' raiding pubs in the city.

The city was hastily decorated: the Albert Memorial clock face was illuminated in celebration and flags and bunting were displayed. At the City Hall the statue of Queen Victoria was draped in bunting, and the Boer War memorial to the Royal Irish Rifles was draped in a large Union Jack. Crowds gathered in the city centre, army bands played and people sang the national anthem. The *Irish*

When the war ended, a floral display was placed before the statue of Queen Victoria, 'In Memory of Our Fallen Heroes'.

MAGNI

News reported that at Castle Place a rousing rendition of 'A Nation Once Again' by a group carrying green flags was heard and a large 'ring o' roses' was performed. The *Belfast News Letter*, recalling the Boer War, commented that not since the relief of Mafeking had the city responded in this way. To the fore of the unionist newspapers' reports of the ceasefire were accounts of the 36th (Ulster) Division and the Battle of the Somme. A service of thanksgiving was held in St Anne's Cathedral, and in several other churches.

 ## Peace Day, 1919

The signing of the peace treaty, the Treaty of Versaillles, took place in June 1919. Under the direction of Lord Curzon, the foreign secretary, the Peace Committee in Britain had met in May to plan the commemoration and ensure that the celebrations were well co-ordinated and choreographed throughout the empire. A victory march in London was organised, and a day of thanksgiving, a river pageant, a day of popular events, and the lighting of bonfires nationwide. Lloyd George, the British prime minister, insisted that each event was to include a tribute to the dead. The architect Edwin Lutyens (1869–1944) was invited by the British government to suggest a design for a suitable memorial, and came up with the idea of a temporary 'catafalque' – in essence, what eventually became the Cenotaph in Whitehall. It was past this temporary structure that London Peace Day parade marched on 19 July 1919.

The exceptionalism that characterised Ulster unionism, so evident in the years before the war, was articulated once more in its Peace Day commemoration. While there were those in Britain who voiced objections to the Peace Day plans, some believing that the time was not apposite, it was for a different reason that Belfast Corporation decided not to take part in the Peace Day celebrations with the rest of the empire but to postpone them until August. In part this decision was reached in order not to clash with the traditional Twelfth of July commemoration. It has also been argued that the delay meant that the Ulster event would not be associated with celebrations in Dublin. Indeed, in many ways, Ulster had two Peace Day commemorations, with the Twelfth of July parades acting as commemorations not only of traditional dates, but also of the First World War. Thus, Twelfth of July celebrations that year were reflective of the atmosphere that the war had helped to generate among Ulster unionists. New arches were erected, covered in images of gallant Ulstermen fighting for the empire and angelic nurses ministering to the wounded, and inviting the people to 'Remember our fallen heroes of the 36th Ulster Division'. Banners portraying the stoical men and women of the 1689 siege of Derry were carried alongside contemporary banners

depicting the new heroes of Ulster, the men who had given their lives for the cause of the empire.

The dead of the 36th Division retrospectively, then, had not died for the Allied war effort but for the freedom of the Protestants of Ulster, and like the executed leaders of the 1916 Easter Rising in Dublin, they became martyrs. This view is reflected in Sir Edward Carson's bitter rhetoric at the Twelfth commemoration in Belfast, reported that day in the *Northern Whig*: 'While the Orange Institution points with melancholy to the records of Thiepval and Messines, those against whose designs they armed in 1912 exult over the records of Easter Week, 1916, in Dublin.'

Ulster's Peace Day, funded to the tune of £12,000 by the Corporation (in addition to voluntary subscriptions), was held the following month, on 9 August.

Ulster's Peace Day, held on 9 August 1919, was declared a public holiday, and between 30,000 and 36,000 people participated in the Belfast parade.

MAGNI

The Garden of Remembrance was originally intended to be surrounded by columns and a balustrade, on which would be placed the four frock-coated statues of municipal gentlemen already in the grounds of the City Hall. However, in the 1920s Alfred Brumwell Thomas was commissioned to redesign the grounds, and was held responsible for the lack of progress because of his absence from Belfast. The architect's relationship with the City Hall had deteriorated after he threatened litigation for the settlement of his fees, and with the Cenotaph and Garden of Remembrance commission he again engaged in disputes with the Corporation over fees and expenses. The whole section was finally completed and unveiled by Field Marshal Viscount Edmund Allenby on Armistice Day, 1929.

MAGNI

The centrepiece of the parade, which began in north Belfast and ended south of the city in Ormeau Park, was the salute, taken by Lord French, at the City Hall. Behind the lord lieutenant, invited guests and the unionist élite, including city councillors led by Lord Mayor J.C. White, reviewed the parade from a specially constructed stand, built to accommodate one thousand people.[14] At a temporary cenotaph erected on the east side of the City Hall, a guard of honour stood with heads bowed around the monument, and 'floral wreaths were piled high about the plinth, and appropriate inscriptions were attached', reported the *Belfast News Letter* on 11 August. On the cenotaph an inscription, raised in gold letters and echoing the inscription on the Whitehall cenotaph, read: 'The glorious dead; in memory of our gallant comrades'.

The bulk of the crowd gathered at the City Hall, watching as the parade took three hours to pass the saluting point. As it did so, the national anthem was played and the crowd cheered the lord lieutenant. 'As a spectacle,' commented the *Belfast News Letter*, 'the march was magnificent, but its true significance lay in the powerful appeal which it made to the emotions.' Sir Edward Carson, arguably the figure whom the crowds most wanted to see, made a short speech praising 'Ulster and her heroes'. The unionist leaders and their guests then retired to the City Hall for lunch.

In a letter to the lord mayor, Lord French, on his retirement as lord lieutenant in 1921, spoke of Ulster's Peace Day:

> I shall always recall the happy and interesting days I spent in Belfast – as the guest of three successive Lord Mayors – with deep pleasure and satisfaction. Of the time of which I speak, one day will ever be foremost in my memory – when the splendid soldiers of Ulster marched past the City Hall in all their unassuming grandeur, in celebration of the Peace which they had helped so much to attain.[15]

MAGNI

First World War Memorials

The war dead are faithfully remembered in the City Hall. In the Entrance Hall bronze tablets commemorate Corporation employees who fought and died in the Great War and a warrior in golden armour, erected by the surviving members of the regiment, commemorates the dead of the North Irish Horse. At the entrance to the Council Chamber an illuminated Roll of Honour records the names of Corporation staff who served in the war, and under the dome, a window, erected by the Corporation and unveiled in June 1920 by Lord French, commemorates the dead of the 36th (Ulster) Division, incorporating George V's tribute to 'the men of Ulster'.

In the West Corridor, where the lord mayor's apartments are situated, hangs a William Conor portrait of Major General Sir Oliver Nugent, commander of the 36th Division, 1915–18, commissioned by the Ulster Division Association, and James Princep Beadle's painting *The Battle of the Somme, 1916*, commissioned by the Ulster Volunteer Force Committee. Beadle, a military artist, often painted war scenes from imagination or with the help of veterans – in this instance, he was assisted by Lieutenant Francis Bodenham Thornley of the 12th Battalion Royal Irish Rifles, the officer who led the men in the attack. The painting represents the 36th Division taking the Schwaben Redoubt on the Somme in October 1916.

The Battle of the Somme by J.P. Beadle

BELFAST CITY COUNCIL

On the landing of the East Staircase a bronze statue of a soldier, on a pedestal of Portland stone, memorialises the men of the 14th Battalion Royal Irish Rifles (the Young Citizen Volunteers) who died during the First World War. The statue was presented to the City Hall in July 1924.

BELFAST CITY COUNCIL

Recent events around the Cenotaph and in the Garden of Remembrance have symbolised the changing political landscape in Northern Ireland. Since the 1990s, members of the Social Democratic and Labour Party have attended Remembrance Sunday commemorations, and Alban Maginnis, the first SDLP lord mayor, became the first nationalist lord mayor to lay a wreath at the Cenotaph. In 2002 Sinn Féin Lord Mayor Alex Maskey broke new ground by laying a wreath at the Cenotaph.

SCENIC IRELAND

The Cenotaph and Garden of Remembrance

Of course, the most significant memorial to the First World War remains the Cenotaph and Garden of Remembrance, designed by Brumwell Thomas, who planned and remodelled the grounds of the City Hall between 1922 and 1924. A veteran of the war himself, he designed the war memorial, which was built by local firm W.J. Campbell and erected between 1925 and 1927. It was unveiled by Field Marshal Viscount Allenby on Armistice Day, 1929, with the 'noble' City Hall providing the impressive backdrop. Dedicated to the 'heroic sons' of Belfast, Allenby's speech, reported that evening in the *Belfast Telegraph*, eulogised the fallen:

Our memorial to them is this Cenotaph – this empty tomb. It holds no mortal remains. All that could die, of those our friends and comrades, lies scattered in lands afar, on the fields where they fought and fell. But the empty tomb is a focus, concentrating the rays of memory; drawing to one point mysterious forces connecting us – in reverence and awe – with the living spirits who have gone beyond reach of our earthly senses.

The following day the *Irish News* commented on this solemn occasion: 'things of stone are yet considered the best monuments to the brave'. Yet there was some dissent about the cost of this war memorial, some critics arguing that the money could have been better spent on the support of war veterans and their families. The newspaper gave voice to the feeling of many nationalists that their contribution to the war, and the contribution of men throughout Ireland, had been overlooked by the Northern Ireland government (established in June 1921), which cast the commemoration in terms of 'men of Ulster' and those 'who defended Ulster when they thought there was a grievance against the Mother Country'. The editorial entreated readers not to forget 'the Leinsters, the Connaughts, the Royal Irish and, indeed, all the Irish battalions whose ranks numbered far more who were Green than those who were Orange', and asked, 'Was their blood-offering less great?'

The Cenotaph is dedicated to the 'men of this city who laid down their lives in the Great War' and incorporates George V's praise of Ulster's soldiers: 'Throughout the long years of struggle which have now so gloriously ended, the men of Ulster have proved how nobly they fight and die.'

The Opening of the Northern Ireland Parliament, 1921

On 22 June 1921 the City Hall was reconfigured as the capital building of the new Northern Ireland state. With the Government of Ireland Act 1920, Belfast became in name what it had been in practice for years, the capital of Northern Ireland. The City Hall was the stage on which the new six-county state was launched by George V, who came to Belfast with Queen Mary to open the Northern Ireland parliament. Earlier, in a more low-key ceremony, Ireland's last lord lieutenant Viscount Fitzalan had formally inaugurated the new parliament on 7 June 1921.

The Imperial Conference had begun in London two days before the Belfast opening, and although ultimately none attended, Northern Ireland's new prime minister, James Craig, invited the dominion premiers to Belfast for the inauguration, stating in a letter to Winston Churchill that their association 'with the Opening of the youngest Parliament within the King's Dominions' would help his efforts to achieve 'a better state of affairs'.

The opening ceremony took a mere fifteen minutes and the royal visit lasted only five hours; its significance lying principally in the king's subsequently oft-quoted appeal to 'all Irishmen to stretch out the hand of forbearance and conciliation, to forgive and forget'.

With Home Rule newly established in Northern Ireland, the British government's Irish strategy was still hard-line, and included consideration of total martial law and an economic blockade against the twenty-six counties. In terms of negotiation with southern Ireland, George V, cast in the role of honest broker by the British and Northern Ireland government, was prompted to use the speech in Belfast 'for a grand gesture of reconciliation'.[16] Significantly, the king's appeal

7 June 1921: Viscount Fitzalan, the last lord lieutenant of Ireland, inspecting troops outside the City Hall on the occasion of the inauguration of the first sitting of the Northern Ireland parliament.

PREVIOUS PAGES:
William Conor had four of his paintings accepted for the 1921 Spring Exhibition of the London National Portrait Society. One was a portrait of Sir James Craig, soon to become Northern Ireland's first prime minister, which Craig bought. On the recommendation of the Belfast artist Sir John Lavery, Conor was appointed to paint a pictorial record of the Opening of the First Northern Ireland Parliament by George V on 22 June 1921 in the Council Chamber of Belfast City Hall. Commenting on an early preparatory pastel sketch, the Marquess of Dufferin and Ava thought that 'it would do no harm to make him [George V] a little taller even if this is not true to life'. Conor's fee, to be collected from subscriptions from members of the Northern Ireland Houses of Commons and Senate, was agreed at £200. In the end however, this amount could not be raised, and he was sent a cheque for £131 6s.

NORTHERN IRELAND ASSEMBLY

for peace 'gave the [British] government the chance to put itself right in the eyes of its critics and exert political pressure on Sinn Féin, where military pressure had, it seemed, met with failure'.[17] Through him, the government found 'the right means of revealing publicly the government's change of front … loyalists would accept from the Crown what they rejected from any other source'.[18] Although the king was arguably sympathetic to the cause of Ulster unionism, his role as mediator was vital, imbuing the message with greater meaning.

According to the historian Charles Townshend, the speech 'provided the necessary cover for the risk of restarting talks in Dublin, and within a fortnight a formal truce was agreed'.[19] It was in terms of the 'King's appeal' that Lloyd George made his subsequent overture to Craig to attend a conference with Eamon de Valera in London.[20] And the Northern Ireland premier was persuaded to accept:

> In view of the appeal conveyed to us by His Majesty, in His Gracious Message on the occasion of the Opening of the Northern Parliament for peace throughout Ireland, we feel that we cannot refuse to accept your invitation to a Conference to discuss how best this can be accomplished.[21]

The royal visit in 1921 is still remembered for the king's appeal for peace, the minutiae of its true origins long forgotten. On another level, however, the official function of George V's visit was purely symbolic; he did not outline the Northern Ireland government's programme for parliament, for example. This was left to Viscount Fitzalan, the lord lieutenant, to announce the following day.

Preparations for the royal visit, while thorough, had been understandably sensitive. In early June, Fitzalan wrote to Craig on a

> very important and difficult point … the absence in the programme of any religious service or prayers. This will have to be arranged for somehow. Stamfordham said the King would insist on it. I told him I assumed it had not been arranged for on account of the difficulty due to the different persuasions etc.

In the end only the Protestant Churches were present at the inauguration to hear the opening prayer, the Nationalist politicians and Catholic hierarchy boycotting the event.

Days before the opening of parliament, the *Belfast Telegraph* outlined previous royal visits to Belfast. However, the forthcoming event was principally set in the context of past unionist demonstrations and incorporated commemorations of Ulster's part in Covenant Day, the Great War, and Peace Day, this element of the familiar allowing those attending the occasion to make a more personal and local connection to the royal visit. Experience of choreographing these earlier demonstrations ensured a well-organised royal visit, which again was presented as an expression of Ulster unionism's enduring place in the empire.

James Craig was of course a consummate past master in stage management,

having honed his skills in Ulster's pre-war anti-Home Rule demonstrations. But the royal event did not come cheap, as he explained to Sir Hamar Greenwood, chief secretary for Ireland:

> There is also the urgent matter of an Entertainment Fund in connection with the Opening Ceremony. I feel bound to have an official Lunch and a Reception later in the day, and to take personally such steps as are necessary in connection with platforms, gangways in the Docks, and decorations as will be worthy of the occasion. Here again, there is no fund [upon] which I can draw.[23]

Fortunately, Craig had not only the Imperial Treasury to appeal to for money, but also benefited from private donations. Belfast was thus bedecked with red, white and blue, with even the straw edging of the royal horses' stalls plaited with patriotic ribbons.

The *Irish Independent* covered the event, reporting that five hundred men were

James Craig at the opening of the Northern Ireland parliament in June 1921. He had written to the lord mayor in May asking for the use of the City Hall: 'If granted, this privilege will be highly appreciated by all concerned. Our new Parliament could not begin its career under better auspices than sit for the first time in your noble building.'[22] The Corporation readily acceded to the request.

GETTY IMAGES

involved in the decoration of Belfast city and the sprucing up of the City Hall itself, and remarked: 'in consequence of the depression in the building trades in recent weeks, the additional work is at the moment particularly welcome'.

The City Hall was of course central to this royal ceremony, as the *Belfast News Letter* reported on 23 June 1921:

> The stately City Hall, the architectural symbol of the progress and greatness of Belfast … is a beautiful building, whose graceful lines – from whatever direction it is seen – are a constant source of pleasure to the citizens. Around it a broad band of well-kept grounds, the bright green of the close-mown grass broken here and there by beds of brilliant flowers, and dotted at regular intervals with the white of marble statues; while on the other side of the broad thoroughfares that surround it on all sides are many tall business premises … the whole enclosing an unrivalled theatre upon which to stage a scene in this great act of Ulster's Constitutional development.

But it was not only the forum and the decorations that so impressed the newspapers – across the board, the press were dazzled by the range of exotic military uniforms, the fine apparel of the ladies and the profusion of gold brocade. As an indication of the large numbers gathered in the city, particularly in front of the City Hall, nurses and members of the ambulance corps lined the royal route (fainting women were singled out in the press as the group most needing their ministrations), while water was supplied by the Irish Temperance Movement and the Water Commissioners, with the help of the Boy Scouts, from whom programmes could be bought for two shillings and six pence. And as they waited, the crowds were treated to an air show by four aeroplanes.

After the ceremonial greeting at the quayside, the royal procession made its way via the Albert Memorial, High Street, Castle Place, Donegall Place and Donegall Square North to the City Hall, the route lined by soldiers of the Norfolk Regiment, the Somersetshire Light Infantry, the Royal Ulster Rifles, the Royal Inniskilling Fusiliers and the Royal Irish Fusiliers. Observers had brought chairs, boxes and even small ladders to enhance their view of the procession, and small children were raised on shoulders. At the City Hall the king was greeted by Northern Ireland's élite – members of the Northern Ireland House of Commons and Senate, the lord mayor and members of the Corporation, as well as others prominent in business and the leaders of the Protestant Churches. In the grounds, specially constructed stands accommodated nearly three thousand onlookers, the majority of whom were members of the public boards, their wives and friends, and war veterans were accorded a special stand in front of the City Hall. In the words of the *Belfast News Letter*:

Lady Craig's diary provides a flavour of the decorations and atmosphere of the royal visit in June 1921:

The King and Queen have the most wonderful reception, the decorations everywhere are extremely well done and even the little side streets that they will never be within miles of are draped with bunting and flags, and the pavement and lampposts painted red white and blue, really most touching, as a sign of their loyalty.[24]

AGNES PEACOCK

George V and Queen Mary arriving at the City Hall for the inauguration of the Northern Ireland parliament in June 1921.

BELFAST TELEGRAPH

At the City Hall the stands erected by the Corporation were crowded, and the scene, with the noble dome of the City Hall towering in the background, and the buildings all round festooned with streamers and gay with flags and bunting, was impressive in the extreme.

The Royal Ulster Rifles formed the guard of honour and, symbolising Ulster's contribution to the war, they were singled out for particular cheering by the assembled crowd. According to the *Belfast News Letter*: 'In them the assembled thousands saluted the Ulster Division, who proved by their courage and devotion to death in those fateful days in France the loyalty of the Imperial province.'

The response of the Belfast press to the royal visit split along predictable political lines. In general, the unionist press followed the official line and took the opportunity to endorse a separate Ulster parliament, while at the same time (and to varying degrees) arguing that southern Ireland could enjoy the same if there were peace. Unsurprisingly, the nationalist *Irish News* on 22 June was highly critical of the British government and the visit. It was particularly critical of the king's speech, arguing in an editorial the following day that Lloyd George's hand was visible in every sentence: 'full of vague professions and pious good wishes'. Taking its tone from a statement issued by the Catholic hierarchy on the eve of the visit, the paper set the opening of the parliament in the context of what it argued had been a year 'of continuous and intolerable persecution directed against the Catholics of Belfast and the surrounding area'. Its main coverage of the royal visit was headlined: 'Four hours of pageantry and feasting: Verbal Flummery: Not an honest word of hope'. During the inspection of the Royal Ulster Rifles, 'a regiment which includes a large proportion of Catholic soldiers', the *Irish News* commented, a section of the crowd sang 'Derry's Walls', although the paper noted that it 'lacked general support and the strains died down after a few minutes'.

The music in the streets found an echo in a more official way in the music played before the royal luncheon in the City Hall. Invited from Dublin to perform, H.W. Hopkins, the director of musicians in Ireland, was reminded by W.B. Spender, Northern Ireland cabinet secretary, that it was 'essential that all the Musicians should be Ulstermen, and should be Loyalists'.

Sectarian tension and prejudice was therefore not hard to locate. On 22 June the *Yorkshire Post* reflected on the partisan nature of the city's decorations: 'Among half-a-dozen arches is one striking archway in Ormeau Avenue, where the drinking fountain forms the central pivot. It bears Orange emblems, and several mottoes, including "Down with Sinn Féin" "Down with traitors".' This was, however, relatively low-level sectarianism, which the strict limiting of alcohol with the closure of all licensed premises on the day of the visit (in addition to the heavy military presence) kept in check, contributing to the good behaviour of the crowd.

Unionist papers made much of the City Hall's role in the ceremony, as the *Belfast News Letter* reported on 23 June:

> Many brilliant functions have been held in the City Hall, many eminent men
> and women have been entertained under its roof, and many famous statesmen
> have spoken within its precincts; but no event previously held there could vie in
> significance and solemnity with the ceremony which was performed yesterday
> by His Majesty the King.

Described in the report as the centre of Ulster loyalty in 1912, the City Hall in 1921 was portrayed as the most appropriate place for 'the scene of a ceremony which will go down to posterity as one of the most momentous events in Irish history'. It was questionable, according to the paper, whether any building in the United Kingdom could 'boast of the possession of a more perfect example of modern architecture':

> Both in its artistic grandeur and its equipment for administrative purposes it is symbolical of the character of the people of the Ulster capital, who combine with their industrial activities a spirit of progress and idealism which finds expression in the happenings and achievements of their daily lives.

The drama unfolding in and around the building added to the royal pageant. The *Belfast News Letter* report glowed with admiration:

> The scene was brilliantly illuminated by the large bronze electrolier of one hundred lights, which is suspended from the centre of the dome, and the effect of the colour scheme was enhanced by the gorgeous uniforms of State officials and the scarlet tunics of a detachment of the Irish Guards.

In the very fabric of the City Hall, unionist reporters saw a force for influencing civic pride, the *Belfast News Letter* commenting:

> Certainly it was in no mean utilitarian spirit that the idea of erecting a City Hall which would be one of the glories of the Empire was conceived by the men who represented the citizens a generation ago. They seem to have realised that such a building would have an enormous influence on the minds and imagination of the people who would come after them, and their bold and farseeing policy has been successful beyond all their anticipations.

Even the *Irish News*, so critical of the visit, was impressed by the internal décor, and its pages made little attempt to disguise the enthusiasm and excitement surrounding the occasion, conceding that 'from a spectacular point of view it was an undoubted success … neither money nor pains were spared in the effort, and on the whole the result was very good'.

Following a sumptuous lunch at the City Hall, the royal procession made its way to the Ulster Hall, scene of so many significant moments in Ulster unionist history, where civic bodies presented loyal addresses. Several leading Unionists had honours and titles bestowed upon them, among them William Pirrie, who was made a viscount, and Lord Mayor William Frederick Coates, who was made a baron.

The 1921 visit was thus dominated by Northern Ireland's unionist and Protestant élites; priority was accorded to the Unionist government, industrialists, civic authorities, and Protestant religious leaders. With northern Catholic

The Ulster Hall in Bedford Street was the scene of many iconic moments in the history of Northern Ireland in the twentieth century.

SCENIC IRELAND

OPPOSITE: The bronze electrolier, suspended from the dome and illuminated by one hundred lights. The total cost of electroliers for the rebuilding was £2,500. The splendour of the marble interior, the stained glass and the crimson carpet all contributed to the richness of the spectacle of the opening of the Northern Ireland parliament in 1921.

MAGNI

This photograph, taken in Southampton in June 1911, shows Lord Pirrie (left) with Captain John Smith (1850–1912) on the White Star Liner *Olympic*. Smith went on to captain the *Titanic* and went down with his ship in 1912. In 1924 Pirrie's body was conveyed on the *Olympic* from New York to Southampton, before his funeral was conducted in London.

Lord William Pirrie (1847–1924) died of pneumonia in June 1924 on a business trip to South America. He was undoubtedly a significant catalyst behind the design and construction of the new City Hall. On the original committee which decided the requirements of the building, he was identified by Sir Daniel Dixon during the Local Government Board Inquiry of 1905, as the person with the 'big ideas' in relation to the City Hall, a role fitting for one of Belfast's wealthiest men. Pirrie's personal rise through the ranks of the titled was intimately connected to the City Hall; he was created a baron on the occasion of the City Hall's opening in August 1906, and during the royal inauguration of the Northern Ireland parliament in 1921 was created a viscount. In addition to his chairmanship of Harland and Wolff, Pirrie was director of nearly forty corporations connected to shipbuilding and the oil industry. According to the *New York Times*, reporting on his death in June 1924, he had an estimated fortune of £500,000,000.

and nationalist élites absenting themselves from the proceedings, the visit sharply underlined the separation of the north from the south and, within the new state, the distance between the Catholic and Protestant communities. It also marked the final act of a movement begun in September 1912 with the signing of the Solemn League and Covenant.

As he told James Craig on his departure, George V's own advisors had been against the Belfast visit, believing that it exposed the king to unnecessary danger. Lady Craig recalled in her diary that she and her husband were informed that the palace had also received 'many letters … begging that Their Majesties should not go over to Ulster'. However, the lord lieutenant assured Craig prior to the visit that 'nothing could exceed [the king's] affability and interest in the arrangements and the whole business'. Given that 1920–22 was a period of extreme violence in the north of Ireland, with 453 deaths, such fears were well founded. And as if to underline the point, the day after the parliament's royal inauguration the Irish Republican Army blew up the train carrying the king's escort, the 10th Hussars, back to Dublin, killing 4 men and 80 horses.

Over a decade after George V's visit, Ulster's local drama was again played out in the City Hall. With the opening of Parliament Buildings, Stormont, only two months away, the Northern Ireland parliament met once more in the City Hall on 30 September 1932, having sat for the previous decade in the Presbyterian Theological College. While the Speaker attempted to note Prime Minister James Craig's thanks to the City Hall for hosting the sitting, Jack Beattie, teacher, trade unionist and member of the Northern Ireland Labour Party, intervened.

He complained that his motion, bringing to the notice of the House of Commons the plight of the unemployed in Northern Ireland, had been refused by the Speaker. Spurred to action, he removed the mace and placed it under the table on which it formally sat. Further angry exchanges led to Beattie seizing the mace again and, proceeding towards the Speaker's chair, he threw it to the floor. Asked to withdraw from the house, he left to the sound of Thomas Henderson, Independent Unionist MP for Belfast Shankill, shouting: 'What about the 78,000 unemployed who are starving?'

That this took place in September 1932 is unsurprising given the prevailing high unemployment and economic slump in Northern Ireland. In the 1930s having no job 'meant often having no income, or at most to have less money than was needed to survive'.[25] Demanding an increase in the relief provided for the unemployed, outdoor relief workers went on strike in October 1932, and outdoor relief riots took place in Belfast in October and November.

The City Hall and the Second World War

The Second World War allowed the Northern Ireland government to consolidate the state's position within the United Kingdom; it also allowed it to establish, in terms of identity, Northern Ireland's oneness with the British Empire and its separateness from Éire. With Éire remaining neutral throughout the hostilities, Northern Ireland and its ports were strategically important to the Allied war effort, and its industries supplied much-needed war material, such as shipping and textiles. The state acted as a base from which the Allies could monitor the dangerous German U-boats patrolling the neutral waters off the Donegal coast, and its strategic importance in the Battle of the Atlantic was something that later commentators were to emphasise constantly. An American naval base was established in Derry, and American airmen were stationed at airfields in counties Antrim and Down.

Northern Ireland's significant wartime role induced confidence amongst unionists that the state would be maintained within the Union following the end of the war. And indeed, participation in the war did create a bond between Britain and Northern Ireland, a bond that was reinforced when Belfast fell victim to German bombing raids in April and May 1941. The Belfast blitz involved four attacks by the Luftwaffe, as a result of which 1,100 people died and 56,000 houses were damaged in addition to numerous factories, businesses and public buildings, including the City Hall. Newtownards, Derry and Bangor were also hit.

The City Hall's stained-glass windows escaped destruction during the bombing of Belfast in May 1941, when the Great Hall was almost completely destroyed. With some foresight, they had been removed for safekeeping, and when the Great Hall was restored they were put back in place.

BELFAST TELEGRAPH

VE Day, 1945

VE Day marked the end of the Second World War, at least in the European theatre. In contrast to the hastily planned celebrations put in place when the First World War ended quite suddenly, the Northern Ireland and British governments knew in advance that this war was likely to end in spring 1945 and they had ample opportunity to organise a fitting response. Sir Crawford McCullagh, Belfast's lord mayor, attended preliminary meetings with the Northern Ireland government in April 1945 to organise the celebrations. In this they may have been particularly anxious to control the celebration, given some minor civil disturbances, largely fuelled by drunkenness, that had erupted at the close of Armistice Day in Belfast in 1918. For the Northern Ireland government, it was important to follow arrangements in Britain as closely as possible and so, in line with British preparations, the Stormont government requested all churches to remain open on VE Day, and the theatres and dance halls were asked to stay open later than usual. VE Day and the day following it were to be a holiday. Church bells throughout Northern Ireland were scheduled to ring at the hour of victory, and a united Protestant service was announced for the Sunday after VE Day, to be held in St Anne's Cathedral.

The *Belfast Telegraph* reported a rush on Allied flags – in particular, the Union Jack, the Stars and Stripes and the Hammer and Sickle. On 8 May, as news of the surrender spread across the city, the *Belfast News Letter* reported the next day, crowds gathered at the City Hall and along Donegall Place and Royal Avenue, singing 'Tipperary' and the favourites of 1918, and 'for hours on end Belfast was a city totally without strangers. Everyone greeted everyone else in communal cheerfulness':

> Youth and age danced together in a surging mass about the city centre and community cheers went up at intervals as brilliant rockets soared above the City Hall, where people from all parts had gathered in festive mood.

At noon the Ulster United Prayer Movement held a victory thanksgiving service in the grounds of the City Hall and during the day crowds gathered to hear Winston Churchill's victory broadcast at 3 p.m. – 'the evildoers lay prostrate before us' – and George VI's broadcast at 9 p.m. Estimated in the unionist press as larger than the throng that had gathered for the signing of Covenant, the density of the crowd brought the south-bound tram traffic to a complete stop – as the *Belfast Telegraph* reported:

> Unforgettable scenes were witnessed in the sun-bathed City Hall grounds, gathering place for huge crowds. Flower beds were trampled underfoot by the

deliriously happy, milling mob. Soldiers, sailors, airmen, WRENS, ATS, WAAFS, American Red Cross workers and civilians made whoopee to music relayed from a battery of loud speakers. They danced Irish jigs, the Victory polka, the Lambeth walk and played 'Kiss in the Ring' and 'Down on the Carpet.' Those who could not find room on the grass clambered to the top of the air raid shelters. There were no strangers in the crowd. All seemed intent on enjoying themselves. They did.

At one point in the afternoon, a British sailor climbed up a static water tank in the City Hall grounds and dived into it. He was joined by others who had stripped down to their underwear for a swim, before clambering out and drying themselves in the sun. With little reverence, another British sailor climbed the statue of Queen Victoria and placed a cigarette between her lips.

On a more solemn note, the *Belfast Telegraph* reported that following Churchill's speech, Sir Crawford McCullagh spoke to the happy crowd:

> Let us remember not only those of this city who lost their lives during the air raids but those who were injured or in any way suffered. We must not forget that we are still at war and much remains to be done before the world is at peace … Certainly celebrate the victory and then go back to work.

For those not at the City Hall, the BBC broadcast Churchill's speech and the

VE Day, 1945
Ulster unionism has always prioritised the local in terms of the empire and this was very much reflected in the ceremonies, centred on the City Hall, which marked the end of the First and Second World Wars. While these events were part of the wider Allied victory celebrations, they were given a very particular local flavour. In this way, the City Hall came to act as the locus for civic patriotism.

BELFAST TELEGRAPH

VE Day celebrations from Belfast, London, Edinburgh, Liverpool and Cardiff, creating the sense of a united nation. As darkness fell, bonfires flared throughout the city. And despite the continued ban on full lighting within a five-mile radius of the coast, Belfast City Hall was floodlit at twenty to eleven, for the first time in over six years. It was a symbolically dramatic moment for the crowd gathered there, and according to the *Belfast Telegraph:*

> A full-throated roar greeted the switching on of the flood-lights which silhouetted the graceful lines of the municipal building against a background of gathering clouds in which glowed a dull red reflection of some of the bonfires which ringed the city. With the playing of the catchy tune 'McNamara's Band' the night's festivities started with a swing.

Just after midnight, the national anthem was played over loudspeakers, followed by three cheers for Churchill and the national anthems of the USA and USSR. Alderman Thomas Henderson then called for a one-minute silence for those who had died in the war, and after the affecting silence, the crowd sang 'Auld Lang Syne'.

 ## Thanksgiving Day

Thanksgiving Day was held the following Sunday, on 12 May 1945, with the state service in St Anne's Cathedral. An all-ticket affair, it was attended by the duke of Abercorn, the Northern Ireland governor, and members of the Northern Ireland government and Belfast Corporation. Separate services were held in Belfast's synagogue and in the Catholic St Peter's Pro-Cathedral. Following the service in St Anne's, a victory parade was held in the city. The parade was made up of Allied soldiers, sailors and airmen, as well as men of the merchant navy, and had a strong local presence with the participation of the Ulster Home Guard, the RUC Special Constabulary, St John Ambulance and Nursing Divisions, and youth organisations. Starting in May's Market, the parade passed the City Hall, where the salute was taken by Admiral

R.H.L. Bevan, RN (retd), flag officer-in-charge, Northern Ireland. He was joined by Sir Basil Brooke, Northern Ireland prime minister, members of the government and the Corporation, and a group of wounded servicemen, special guests of the Corporation. The crowds cheered as the parade passed the City Hall and the massed bands of the RUC and the Ulster regiments played 'Hearts of Oak':

> Still Britain shall triumph, her ships plough the sea,
> Her standard be justice, her watchword 'Be free',
> Then cheer up, my lads, with our hearts let us sing,
> Our soldiers, our sailors, our statesmen, and King.

After the parade, Alderman W.F. Neill held a reception in the Banqueting Hall.

On 8 May 1945, after a black-out of over six years, ecstatic crowds celebrating the end of the war cheered as the City Hall was floodlit once again.

MAGNI

VJ Day, 1945

On 15 August 1945 the City Hall played a central role in the events that marked the end of the war in Japan. Following the announcement by British Prime Minister Clement Attlee on 14 August that the Japanese had surrendered, bonfires were lit around Belfast as night fell and crowds of people, some wearing their pyjamas under their coats and led by a flute band, assembled at the City Hall to celebrate. The revellers were reluctant to leave and they danced and sang around the City Hall until the early hours. 'To thousands,' wrote the *Belfast Telegraph* on 16 August, 'the day meant fathers, sons, and brothers would soon return from battle in Burma and the Far East.'

At noon the next day an open-air service of thanksgiving was held in the City Hall's grounds, and in the evening, as servicemen climbed lampposts and clambered over the statue of Queen Victoria, crowds waited to hear the king's speech, which was relayed over loudspeakers, and cheered wildly when he declared, 'The war is over.' In his speech, Sir Crawford McCullagh, the lord mayor, drew special attention to those who had suffered as a result of the blitz but continued: 'By all means let us rejoice in the victory won. We have a right to be proud to belong to a great nation and to have played our part in the past struggle.'

After the VE parade in Belfast on 12 May 1945, a reception was held in the Great Hall.

MAGNI

Second World War Memorials

By comparison with the number of memorials dedicated to the First World War, the physical monuments at the City Hall devoted solely to the Second World War are few. The 1939–45 war was a different type of conflict, one which brought the horrors of war to the doorsteps of ordinary people, and demanded a different form of remembrance. It is fitting in the context of a non-combatants' war that, rather than a range of dedicated material reminders, the City Hall itself became the site for civic patriotism and a venue where the whole city could gather to remember and celebrate their collective survival.

The Cenotaph and the Garden of Remembrance, which was created to commemorate the dead of the Great War, now became a site to remember also those

American troops landed in Belfast at Dufferin Quay on 26 January 1942, as the band of the Royal Ulster Rifles played 'The Star-Spangled Banner'.

BELFAST TELEGRAPH

The American Expeditionary Force commemorative stone column, sculpted by local stonemasons Purdy and Millard, was unveiled by the Northern Ireland governor, the duke of Abercorn, in January 1943. William Baird, managing director of the *Belfast Telegraph*, had a one-twelfth scale model of the memorial sculpted from an off-cut of the monument and sent to President Franklin D. Roosevelt as a memento of the unveiling.

BELFAST CITY COUNCIL

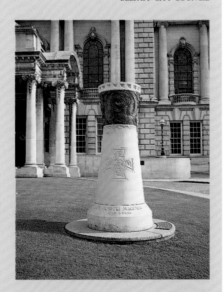

The memorial for Leading Seaman James Magennis VC, erected in 1999.

BELFAST CITY COUNCIL

Canadian Air Cadets visit the American Expeditionary Force commemorative column in August 1959.

BELFAST TELEGRAPH

who died in the later war. In the Entrance Hall, alongside the First World War memorial tablet, hangs a bronze tablet commemorating the members of the Belfast Civil Defence Services who died in the 1941 air raids. And in 1962 a commemorative window to those of the North Irish Horse who died in the Second World War, by the artist John Calderwood, was installed in the City Hall.

Also, reflecting Northern Ireland's position as a staging post for Allied troops, a memorial in front of the City Hall marks the arrival of the American Expeditionary Force in Belfast in January 1942. The unveiling of the stone column, on 26 January 1943, was followed by a march past of US army, marines, sailors and nurses, accompanied by the massed bands of the Royal Ulster Rifles and the Royal Irish Fusiliers. As the *Belfast Telegraph* reported:

> Ten thousand citizens crammed the grounds and approaches of the City Hall to witness the occasion, and every vantage point, including windows, statues and the roof of the City Hall itself, was occupied.

Those reviewing the march past included the Northern Ireland prime minister, J.M. Andrews, Sir Percy James Grigg, the British secretary of state for war, Lord Mayor Sir Crawford McCullagh, and Major General Russell P. Hartle, the commander of American forces at the time of their arrival in Northern Ireland.

In 1945 General Dwight D. Eisenhower inspected a guard of honour at the column and it was thereafter often referred to locally as the 'Eisenhower stone', many people believing erroneously that it was erected in his honour. It was rededicated in November 1995 by President Bill Clinton.

And in 1999, Leading Seaman James Magennis, the only serviceman from Northern Ireland to be awarded the Victoria Cross during the Second World War, was honoured with a memorial in the City Hall grounds, a bronze and stone plinth in the shape of a ship's capstan.

Royal Visits

The Second World War had brought rationing and bombing to Northern Ireland. In such circumstances, the desire to celebrate the end of hardship and uncertainty was understandable. The City Hall had played a central role in the celebrations of the summer of 1945, with none more significant than the visit of George VI, Queen Elizabeth and Princess Elizabeth on 18 July 1945, during their royal tour celebrating the end of war in Europe. The king and queen had visited Northern Ireland in 1942 on a morale-boosting tour focused particularly around the military, war industries and war workers. In 1945 the royal party stayed at Government House in Hillsborough, and then travelled to Belfast's Musgrave Dock to inspect a naval guard of honour before visiting Parliament Buildings, Stormont. After the king's speech to the Northern Ireland House of Commons and the Senate, an investiture ceremony was conducted. The royal party then drove to the City Hall for lunch, where George VI inspected an RUC guard of honour.

Crowds gathered around the City Hall, some climbing the surrounding lampposts to get a better view of the royal family. The close of this busy day was a visit to Botanic Gardens, where a garden party for war workers was held. In the evening, the *Belfast News Letter* reported on 18 July 1945, the royals attended a private dinner party in Government House in Hillsborough. In 1952, when Princess Elizabeth acceded to the throne, the *Belfast Telegraph* believed that the 1945 royal visit had been the most exciting for the city:

> Victory had been won. The long night of the war was over and Ulster put on her best finery to give the King, who was accompanied by the Queen and Princess Elizabeth, an unforgettable reception.

TOP: The Lord Mayor, Sir Crawford McCullagh, receiving Princess Elizabeth at the City Hall, 19 March 1946.

MIDDLE: Princess Elizabeth with the Lord Mayor and the Town Clerk, John Dunlop.

RIGHT: Princess Elizabeth inspecting the RUC under the command of District Inspector Murphy.

PRONI

In the years after the Second World War, Elizabeth II made several visits to Northern Ireland. That the governor of Northern Ireland, Lord Granville, was her uncle (married to her aunt Lady Rose Bowes-Lyon) may have encouraged her to make such trips. When he retired as governor in 1952 that family connection with Northern Ireland was severed.

1946

1949

TOP: Princess Elizabeth and the duke of Edinburgh being received by the Lord Mayor, Sir William Neill, MP, on their visit to Belfast in May 1949.
PRONI

MIDDLE: Princess Elizabeth and the duke of Edinburgh arriving at the City Hall.
PRONI

BOTTOM: Princess Elizabeth signing the Freeman's Roll in the Council Chamber.
PRONI

In 1953 ceremonial bonfires were lit across Great Britain in celebration of the coronation of the new queen, Elizabeth II. On 2 June, Belfast's celebration of the coronation began at the City Hall, with the bands of the 6th Battalion Royal Ulster Rifles (TA) and the pipes and drums of the Queen's University Training Corps (TA) providing a military fanfare. Northern Ireland's ceremonial torch was lit by Deputy Lord Mayor Henry Holmes at the City Hall, and then carried in relay by 135 Boy Scouts along a designated route to the coronation bonfire on top of Cave Hill.

During a three-day coronation visit to Northern Ireland a month later, on 2 July, the City Hall played host to Elizabeth II and the duke of Edinburgh.

Crowds waited for hours outside the City Hall in order to see the arrival of the royal party, the *Belfast Telegraph* observing that with 'snatches of song and good humoured banter the thousands whiled away the waiting time'. The organisers of the royal itinerary must have panicked when a widespread electricity failure affected the city between 11.20 a.m and 1.30 p.m. In the grounds of the City Hall, stands were erected to accommodate a thousand guests, and were lined along the footpath of the carriageway. In the end, the long wait for the arrival of the royal party proved too much for one member of the Territorial Army, who fainted, as the *Belfast News Letter* reported the next day:

But in a matter of seconds and almost unnoticed he was rushed into a room for attention and the gap in the ranks filled before her Majesty appeared at the steps rising to the porch.

An investiture ceremony was held in the City Hall, with the lord mayor, Percival Brown, receiving a knighthood. Lunch was held in the Banqueting Hall for six hundred guests, drawn from the Northern Ireland government, the Belfast Corporation, public bodies, the Protestant Churches, and representatives of the city's industry and commerce. The *Belfast News Letter* report continued:

> One thousand roses in red, gold and yellow decorated the tables, which were traced with selaginella, and the Irish Guards orchestra, in red tunics, played on the platform, the base of which was covered with flowers and foliage.

This was a unionist-dominated occasion, with the *Irish News* reporting the following day that the ten Irish Labour Party members were denied tickets to the lunch and were refused an allocation of tickets for the stands in the grounds.

TOP: Elizabeth II and the duke of Edinburgh at the City Hall, 2 July 1953, during the queen's coronation tour. Memories of the Second World War were recalled on this royal visit by the *Belfast News Letter*:

> Yesterday's visit to the City Hall by our young Queen has added a bright page to the records of royal interest in our civic life, and it must have given satisfaction to the Lord Mayor and his colleagues that their banqueting hall, which was struck and gutted by enemy bombs in the last war, was restored in time to make a suitable setting for the occasion.

PRONI

BOTTOM: The theme of the Second World War was underlined again at Balmoral Show Grounds, where the young queen reviewed ex-servicemen and women.

PRONI

BELFAST TELEGRAPH

Responses to royal visits were not always enthusiastic. In 1977 the jubilee clock, planted in the City Hall grounds, was vandalised. Here workmen display the damage.

The John Luke Mural

In terms of additions to the fabric of the City Hall's interior, the most prominent feature of the Rotunda remains the John Luke mural, unveiled in May 1952 by Dame Dehra Parker. As part of the Festival of Britain Northern Ireland 1951, Luke was commissioned by the Council for the Encouragement of Music and the Arts (the forerunner to the Arts Council of Northern Ireland) to paint a mural in Belfast City Hall that would represent the history of Belfast and its industries. The Festival of Britain, organised by the post-war Labour government, was ostensibly convened to commemorate the centenary of the Great Exhibition of 1851. With the intention of boosting the nation's morale, it succeeded, according to one commentator, in proving to the British population that they still possessed a 'vital and vigorous culture', were 'still at peace' with themselves and were 'secure in [their] heritage'.[26]

In the period following the Second World War, Belfast's traditional industries were thriving, due to the boost of war-time production. Politically, the late 1940s was a period in which the Northern Ireland state was striving to create a more secure future for itself against the background of an uncertain past and this appeared to have been achieved by the early 1950s. This seemed a positive period of economic growth for the state, with the Korean War prolonging the economic war-time benefits by giving Northern Ireland's traditional industries of shipbuilding and linen manufacture a new lease of life. The Festival of Britain thus provided an opportunity for the Northern Ireland government to promote the northern state as a modern industrial centre.

The high-profile City Hall mural represented the peak of John Luke's career. Although responsible for significant murals in the Rosemary Street Masonic Hall and in Millfield Technological College, Luke's City Hall mural was the first such work in Belfast, articulating, as officially commissioned murals often do, the city's municipal and industrial history. Here, the central figure is of Sir Arthur Chichester reading the town charter. Lord deputy of Ireland from 1604 to 1614, Chichester, as a historical icon, personifies the dominance of Protestant planter heritage in Northern Ireland, and St Anne's Church figures prominently, identifying Protestantism as the dominant religion. The mural also represents the linen and shipbuilding industries, so vital to Belfast's advancement.

That Luke's work reflected such an overwhelmingly Protestant heritage is due to the character of a city whose main industries were dominated by Protestants and whose history was rooted in the plantations. As one writer has noted, 'Luke chose political, economic, religious, and social icons based on their inherent merit and value to the city.'[27] Above all, the Luke mural encapsulates a sense of civic pride in the city's history and industries, echoing and reinforcing the dominant symbolic concerns of the City Hall from its inception.

PREVIOUS PAGES:
John Luke's mural depicts scenes from Belfast's history and features Sir Arthur Chichester reading the town charter, awarded by James I in 1613. Commissioned to mark the 1951 Festival of Britain Northern Ireland, the mural bore testimony to the fact that the city (and indeed the City Hall itself) had, despite the blitz, survived the war.

BELFAST CITY COUNCIL

On 6 August 2001, Fred Johnston wrote about the City Hall in his 'Irishman's Diary' in the *Irish Times*:

I remember vividly the starlings around Belfast City Hall, viewed in their swirling madness from the top deck of a growling bus, and the year [1964] Queen's University students climbed out on the greeny dome and painted on its front, in enormous white letters, the initials of their outrageous rag-week magazine, PTQ. The lettering could be seen all the way up Royal Avenue … I hadn't been in the grand and grandiose City Hall for many years. My father took me there one day and showed me, under glass, the Covenant, signed in blood. The City Hall, in many ways, is Belfast. There is something proud, arrogant, beautiful and sad about its size, its marble, its statues, its pictures, its gleaming halls. Inside, you look up at the dome, a sort of secular St Peter's, though that description probably doesn't occur to too many people walking under it. The City Hall is about Belfast's glory days, days of powerful industry, of mills, full order-books in the shipyard, the largest rope works in the world, my grandfather as secretary of East Belfast Constitutional Workingmen's Club, stiff collars, the Titanic, rectitude, an empire to serve.

In 1970 industrial cleaners were hired to disperse the starlings with sirens and searchlights in order to clean the building.

A Site for Civic Protest

Within days of its opening, as noted previously, the City Hall was established as a rallying point – a trend that has continued to the present day. In December 1919, for example, large numbers of unemployed people gathered there to press the Corporation to take action to alleviate their distress, and they gathered there again, in 1926, before marching to the Lisburn Road to protest to the Board of Guardians about the inadequate levels of relief for the unemployed. And in the second half of the twentieth century, before the onslaught of deepening conflict, the City Hall became a focal point for the civil rights protests of the 1960s.

A decade before the premiership of Captain Terence O'Neill civic relations were harmonious between Dublin and Belfast. The lord mayor of Dublin, Bernard Butler, TD, and his lady mayoress visited Belfast City Hall and Lord Mayor James Norritt in 1953.

PRONI

As a sign of the thawing of sectarian tensions in Northern Ireland, in 1962 William Philbin, Catholic bishop of Down and Connor, accepted an invitation from Lord Mayor Martin Wallace to a reception in the City Hall. This gesture of reconciliation was in keeping with other initiatives that heralded the O'Neill era.

In 1963, on the death of Pope John XXIII, a pontiff whose attempts to heal rifts between Catholics and Protestants were acknowledged worldwide and who had instigated Vatican II, Belfast's lord mayor, William Jenkins, sent condolences to Bishop Philbin, and the City Hall lowered its flag to half-mast as a mark of respect. The next day five hundred people, led by the Reverend Ian Paisley, protested at the City Hall against this gesture of sympathy – a sign of the difficulties to come.

From the beginning of the Troubles, the City Hall has been a site for protest and conflict – often one group's attempts at preventing another reaching the building itself. It has also been the venue for groups, such as Witness for Peace and the Peace People, which advocated peace and reconciliation.

On 5 October 1968 civil rights campaigners and the RUC clashed at a civil rights march in Derry and two days of rioting ensued. On 9 October three thousand Queen's University students (and about twenty members of academic staff) attempted to march to Belfast City Hall in protest. When the police blocked their progress to avoid a clash with a counter-demonstration led by Ian Paisley, the marchers held a three-hour sit-down in Linenhall Street. From this initial protest the People's Democracy was born. A week later, on 16 October, two thousand Queen's University students did succeed in marching on City Hall in support of civil rights. And on New Year's Day 1969 civil rights protestors set off from the City Hall to march to Derry. It was this march that was attacked at Burntollet, sparking communal violence and the first deaths of the Troubles.

As attempts were made to find a political settlement in Northern Ireland, Belfast City Hall continued to maintain its position as a place of civic protest. In November 1985, 200,000 unionists rallied in front of City Hall to protest against the signing of the Anglo-Irish Agreement, an echo of the crowds that gathered for the signing of the Solemn League and Covenant in 1912. The slogan of the unionist campaign, 'Ulster Says No', was used extensively throughout Northern Ireland on local government buildings. A large banner hanging on the front of the City Hall remained in place for many years, with its more local 'Belfast Says No', being adapted in Christmas 1987 to 'Belfast Says Noel'.

The rallies of the last decade reflect the changing fortunes of the peace process and the response of citizens. At the close of the twentieth century, the Northern Ireland Committee of the Irish Congress of Trade Unions (NIC ICTU) was the principal organiser of rallies at the City Hall, articulating public attitudes to the evolving, frequently shaky, peace process.

NICRA

Civil rights protesters from Queen's University were prevented from reaching the City Hall on 9 October 1968, and they staged a sit-down protest in Linenhall Street.

As a protest against the Anglo-Irish Agreement Belfast City Council refused to set a rate, and in February 1987 they were fined £25,000 by the Belfast High Court for failing to conduct normal business. This photograph of an anti-Agreement rally shows the iconic 'Belfast Says No' banner on the City Hall, part of the unionist campaign against the Agreement. The photograph also shows the 'Unionist Solidarity' banner. In 1986 the campaign adopted the symbolism of the Polish Solidarity movement and the image of democratic legitimacy in the face of oppressive government.
SCENIC IRELAND

William Craig, former Northern Ireland government minister and leader of Ulster Vanguard, helped organise a two-day strike against the suspension of the Northern Ireland government and the introduction of Direct Rule in March 1972. Here supporters listen to his address at a City Hall rally.

GETTY IMAGES

In February 1996 the IRA ceasefire, called in August 1994, ended abruptly with the bombing of Canary Wharf in London. In response, fifteen thousand people attended an ICTU lunchtime rally at Belfast City Hall, under the slogan 'Ceasefire Now – Give Us Back Our Peace'. Although the IRA announced another ceasefire in July 1997, the peace was not sustained, and as killings once more featured in the Northern Ireland news, the ICTU organised a series of peace rallies in Derry, Enniskillen, Lurgan, Antrim and Omagh, culminating in a major rally at the City Hall in January 1998. 'The force of argument has to replace the argument of force,' argued Frank Bunting, chairman of NIC ICTU. Controversially, some sections of the crowd displayed anti-unionist and anti-loyalist banners, causing Ulster Unionist Party and Progressive Unionist Party leaders to leave the event when the protesters refused to lower them.

In January 2002, in response to the UDA murder of Catholic postman Daniel McColgan, an anti-sectarianism rally organised by the ICTU was supported by an

BELFAST TELEGRAPH

In December 1977 a rally at the City Hall welcomed home Betty Williams and Mairead Corrigan of the Peace People, who had been awarded the 1976 Nobel Peace Prize. In his presentation speech in the University Festival Hall, Oslo, Egil Aarvik, vice-chairman of the Norwegian Nobel Committee, explained why the women had been honoured: 'We admire Betty Williams and Mairead Corrigan for tackling so fearlessly the perilous task of leading the way into no-man's land, in the cause of peace and reconciliation.' Mairead Corrigan's sister, Anne Maguire, and her children were hit by a wounded gunman's getaway car. Three of the children died and Anne Maguire was badly injured. Spurred on by the tragedy, Corrigan and Williams founded the Northern Ireland Peace Movement, which later became the Peace People. In its early phase the organisation managed to glean cross-community support, but as time went on, this support could not be sustained in the face of widespread violence and internal tensions. Despite the prestigious award, Belfast City Council voted against giving the women the freedom of the city or arranging a civic reception for them, and the lord mayor, James Stewart, excused himself from the platform outside the City Hall where the crowds greeted Williams, Corrigan and their fellow leader, Ciaran McKeown. Instead, Stewart sent a letter of congratulations to both women and invited them for an informal meeting in the lord mayor's parlour, and while Mairead Corrigan attended, Betty Williams did not.

A 1993 poster for a high-profile republican rally outside the City Hall, symbolising the shift in power in the city's politics. The first republican rally had been held in July 1991. By the later 1990s Sinn Féin was the largest single party in Belfast.

SINN FÉIN

The bombing of the City Hall in May 1994 was the first significant bomb damage the building had suffered since the blitz in 1941.

BELFAST TELEGRAPH

estimated thirty thousand in the grounds of City Hall. On the platform, Northern Ireland's first and deputy first ministers, David Trimble and Mark Durkan, were joined by the minister of finance Sean Farren, minister of arts Michael McGimpsey and minister of education Martin McGuinness. As the *Irish Times* commented on 19 January 2002:

> The civic community expressed its abhorrence and revulsion of sectarianism in society yesterday. The protests were peaceful. They send a powerful message to all of the paramilitaries. The people, by referendum, decided to pursue the path of peace and politics and, despite the apparently insurmountable difficulties, they still want to reach that goal.

Two years later, in January 2004, following a series of racially motivated attacks in the city, a rally against racism was organised outside Belfast City Hall by the Anti-Racism Network, with a second rally following in November of that year. Uniting trade unionists, politicians, representatives of welfare associations for people of ethnic background and the general public, the City Hall once more provided a platform for civic protest.

The Northern Ireland Committee of the Irish Congress of Trade Unions has provided civic leadership for Northern Ireland in protests against sectarianism, racism and war.

IRISH TIMES

Thousands gathered at the City Hall in January 2002 to protest against sectarianism, and to support the struggle for peace.

IRISH TIMES

Since 1998 the City Hall has acted as the venue for St Patrick's Day events. In 2006 the new focus of St Patrick's Day will be a celebration in the rejuvenated Custom House Square, a return to the civic venue of the early twentieth century.

SCENIC IRELAND

The Lord Mayor's Show is a one-day event that marks the end of the lord mayor's term in office and is intended as a broader civic celebration for Belfast's citizens. In recent years it has taken on a carnival air, with the lord mayor in his carriage and a themed parade snaking through the city and past the City Hall. In May 1998 it was aptly themed as 'City of Dreams', coming as it did the day after the referendum on the Good Friday Agreement. As the *Belfast Telegraph* reported: 'Back out on the busy streets of Belfast the mood was jovial – thanks in part to the Lord Mayor's Show which somehow seemed to scoop up and capture the mood of optimism that was tangible as word of the 71% Yes vote filtered through.' In 2006, while the City Hall celebrates its centenary, the Lord Mayor's Show will celebrate its golden jubilee.

Alban and Carmel Maginnis in the lord mayor's carriage in May 1998. Alban Maginnis of the SDLP was the first nationalist lord mayor of Belfast.

BELFAST TELEGRAPH

Traditional floats pass the City Hall during the Lord Mayor's Show in May 1966.

BELFAST TELEGRAPH

Today the Show is a more carnivalesque and multi-cultural affair.

BELFAST TELEGRAPH

At the start of the peace process, people gathered at
the Cenotaph to remember those who had died in
the Enniskilllen bombing in 1987.

BELFAST TELEGRAPH

Conclusion

The celebrations for the opening of Belfast City Hall in August 1906 were capped with a lavish ball, filling the building with 2,500 guests. A flavour of that occasion was given in a description of a lord mayor's soiree by Robert Johnstone in a guide to Belfast published in 1909:

> Seen on such an occasion with the blaze from its many fine electroliers lighting up the snowy alabaster and delicate green of its elaborate decorations, and with its crowded floor gay with brilliant dresses, and rich with scarlet uniforms and crimson robes, the most captious critic will confess that it is a noble hall of state, and worthy of the municipal palace of a great and flourishing city.[28]

It was a spectacle, that 20,000 visitors came to view in the two days following its opening; a tradition maintained to the present in daily tours of the building, evidence of Belfast's growing popularity as a tourist destination. 'Its creation,' proclaimed the *Irish Builder* on 11 August 1906, 'heralds the coming of a new era, when the city will recognise that only in art can human consciousness find its supreme expression, and that man cannot live and be long satisfied by trade alone.' Whether such high ideals have been consistently maintained over the century since the City Hall opened is a matter for debate, but in the recent civic rallies held there Belfast's citizens have proven themselves capable of rising above serious ordeals and bearing witness to great humanity.

This entrance on the eastern façade was used principally by guests attending City Hall functions. The vista has since been altered by the repositioning of the *Titanic* and Boer War memorials to this side of the building.

MAGNI

141

The US presidential visit in November 1995 was the first of several visits
Bill Clinton made in order to support the peace process.

SCENIC IRELAND

PAULA McELROY

President Clinton
Belfast City Hall
30 November 1995
6.00 pm

Design: Paula McElroy Year 2 BA (Hons) Visual Communication University of Ulster

LINEN HALL LIBRARY

PRESIDENT and MRS. CLINTON

City Centre • Belfast • November 30th • 1995 • 6 p.m.

These posters were created for the Clinton visit. In the his keynote speech
at Mackie's engineering factory in Belfast, the US president said: 'You, the
vast majority of Protestant and Catholic alike, must not allow the ship of
peace to sink on the rocks of old habits and hard grudges.'

In the summer of 1910 the band of the Royal Irish Constabulary agreed to perform once a week in the grounds of Belfast City Hall. Nearly a century later, thousands attended an open-air concert in the grounds.

Begun in 2001, the BBC Proms in the Park has become a popular event in Belfast. In September 2005 it was attended by an estimated five thousand people and broadcast popular classical music to millions from the Donegall Square grounds. It featured the Ulster Orchestra conducted by Belfast-born Kenneth Morgan, percussionist Evelyn Glennie, harpist Cliona Davis, the City of Derry Youth Choir and Codetta.

BBC NORTHERN IRELAND

While a remarkable building in its own right, over its one hundred years the City Hall has accrued layers of meaning, as it changed and adapted to the life and times of its Belfast citizens. At a local level the people have made it their own – by the erection of statues, and the placing of stained-glass commemorations and memorabilia – to reflect their city's unique social, cultural and political experiences.

At the turn of the twentieth century Belfast's municipal aspiration was to build a permanent symbol of its industrial and mercantile success, one which would represent it fittingly within the British Empire. Its planning and construction were part of the development of and investment in Belfast's urban landscape. A century later Belfast is witnessing new investment and development, from the Waterfront Hall built in 1997 by Belfast City Council, an icon of the city's renewal as a venue for major international artists and large-scale conferences

Additions to the City Hall have sometimes caused controversy. In September 2002, Alex Maskey, the first republican lord mayor, hung the Tricolour in the lord mayor's parlour. Against his argument that this was a move towards equality, Unionists objected to what they saw as the display of a flag of a foreign country.

PACEMAKER

alike, to the city's landmark millennium project, the Odyssey Arena, erected near the old Harland and Wolff shipyard on the waterfront. This regeneration has created its own momentum, with the £300 million Victoria Square retail development, opposite the old Town Hall. In terms of scale and ambition, the greatest of all these schemes must be Titanic Quarter, the biggest mixed-use waterfront development in Europe. On the 185-acre site of the Harland and Wolff shipyard, where many of the world's greatest liners, including the *Titanic*, were built and launched, the £1 billion development will see the creation of a striking array of

apartments, offices, restaurants, hotels, marinas and visitor attractions. The first stage of the multi-million pound Northern Ireland Science Park has already been established in the area. It is perhaps fitting that the Titanic Quarter should be one of Belfast's flagship developments at the start of the twenty-first century, given that Lord Pirrie, a driving force behind the City Hall and the great liners *Olympic* and *Titanic*, was also chairman of Harland and Wolff.

Belfast City Hall is embedded in its historical setting, an expression of the Victorian industry and ambition which built it, but it has risen above its origins to encompass the whole civic community. It remains a building which, from its inception, has reflected civic Belfast to itself, and symbolised the city to the wider world. Since the peace process was established, little more than a decade or so ago, Belfast has seen a remarkable transformation. In many ways, City Hall has been at the forefront of that change: the now famous speech of President Clinton, which gave such impetus to the peace process, was delivered in its grounds in November 1995. Here, in the heart of the city, outside the building that came to symbolise the pride and seemingly limitless ambition of Victorian and Edwardian Belfast, came the defining moment of Belfast's latest resurgence, triggering a new and equally spectacular era of growth.

SCENIC IRELAND

Born in east Belfast in May 1946, George Best was considered by many to have been the most naturally gifted footballer of his generation. One of the first sportsmen to become a modern superstar, Best's glory years were with Manchester United, winning the League Championship in 1965 and 1967, and the European Cup in 1968. He was made English and European Footballer of the Year in 1968. Best's personal problems with alcohol are well documented, but his own wish was that he would be remembered for the football. When he died on 25 November 2005 football fans throughout the world paid tribute to him. Many of them travelled to Northern Ireland to join the estimated thirty thousand who attended his funeral service in Parliament Buildings, Stormont, and the tens of thousands more who lined the route of the funeral cortège. The photograph shows the tributes to George Best left outside the City Hall by the people of Belfast in the week following his death.

)ON GILLESPIE

On 19 December 2005 Shannon Sickles and Grainne Close exchanged vows in Belfast City Hall. History was made in Belfast as the City Hall provided the venue for the first civil partnership ceremony for gay couples to take place in the United Kingdom.

MARK PIERCE/PACEMAKER

FT: Fireworks at the millennium celebrations

:NIC IRELAND

NOTES

1 Cited in Sybil Gribbon, 'An Irish City: Belfast 1911', in David Harkness and Mary O'Dowd (eds), *The Town in Ireland* (Belfast: Appletree Press, 1981), p. 204

2 *The City Hall of the County Borough of Belfast: A Monograph in Three Chapters* (Belfast: W. & G. Baird, 1906), p. 47

3 Ian Budge and Cornelius O'Leary, 'The Age of Consolidation', in *Belfast: Approach to Crisis. A Study of Belfast Politics, 1613–1970* (London: Macmillan, 1973), p. 133. *Dublin Gazette*, 22 September 1905, p. 1198

4 Sub-committee members Lord Mayor William McCammond, Lord Mayor elect William Pirrie, Alderman R.J. McConnell (chairman), Alderman Thomas Brown (vice chairman of the improvement committee) and Alderman Lavens M. Ewart, in conjunction with the city surveyor

5 Meeting of the Sub General Purposes and Improvement Committee, 21 March 1896, PRONI LA/7/16AB/3/4

6 Meeting of Council in Committee, 25 June 1896, PRONI LA/7/16AB/3/4

7 Andrew Trimble, *Guide to Belfast* (Belfast: W. & G. Baird, 1911), p. 14

8 ibid.

9 Myrtle Hill, *Women in Ireland: A Century of Change* (Belfast: Blackstaff Press, 2003), p. 62

10 Extract from Cabinet Publicity Committee, 7 December 1961, PRONI CAB/9B/2/1

11 Keith Jeffery, *TLS*, quoted on jacket of Frank McGuinness, *Observe the Sons of Ulster Marching towards the Somme* (London: Faber & Faber, 1986)

12 Paul Fussell, *The Great War and Modern Memory* (Oxford: Oxford University Press, 1975), p. 12

13 Meeting of Council in Committee, 19 July 1916, PRONI PRONI LA/7/16AB/3/4

14 Minutes of the Improvement Committee, 29 July 1919, PRONI LA/2EB/73

15 Letter Lord French to lord mayor, 11 May 1921; General Purpose Committee, 27 May 1921, PRONI LA/2EB/81

16 *Thomas Jones Whitehall Diary: Ireland 1918–25*, ed. Keith Middlemas (Oxford: Oxford University Press, 1971), vol. 3, p. 77

17 D. George Boyce, *Nineteenth-Century Ireland: The Search for Stability* (Dublin: Gill and Macmillan, 1990), p. 269

18 Oliver MacDonagh, *Ireland* (New Jersey: Prentice Hall, 1968), p. 88

19 Charles Townshend, *Ireland. The Twentieth Century* (London: Arnold, 1998), p. 104

20 Lady Craig's diary, 26 June 1921, PRONI D/1415/B/38/1–162. *The Times*, 23 June 1921, printed Lloyd George's letter to Craig following the visit: 'I hope and believe their influence and example will assist to set the whole of Ireland long upon the path of practical co-operation, which alone can lead to the realisation of Irish ideals and the security of Irish interests. The [Better] Government of Ireland act has put the future of Ireland in the hands of her own people, provided only that Southern Ireland renounces its claim to secession from the Empire.' PRONI D/1415/A/11

21 Craig to Lloyd George, 28 June 1921, PRONI CAB/4/6

22 Letter James Craig to Belfast lord mayor, General Purpose Committee, 27 May 1921, PRONI LA/7/2EB/81

23 Craig to Greenwood, 27 April 1921, PRONI PM/1/71

24 Lady Craig's diary, 20–22 June 1921, PRONI D/1415/B/38/1–162

25 Bill Rolston, *An Oral History of Belfast in the 1930s* (Belfast: Blackstaff Press, 1987), p. 18

26 As the king said at St Paul's Cathedral: 'This Festival of Britain has been planned, like its great predecessor, as a visible sign of national achievement and confidence', quoted in *Belfast News Letter*, 4 May 1951; Kenneth O. Morgan (ed.), *Oxford History of Britain* (Oxford: Oxford University Press, 1993), p. 637

27 Nick Doughty, 'Dirty Old Town? The Belfast Murals of John Luke', unpublished MA dissertation, 1999, Queen's University Belfast, p. 28

28 Robert Johnstone, *Handbook and Guide to Belfast and North-East Ireland* (Belfast, 1909), p. 18

A NOTE ON SOURCES:

In addition to specific books on Belfast by W.A. Maguire and Jonathan Bardon, and a broader literature on urban history, there is a wealth of material on Belfast City Hall waiting for researchers to delve into in Belfast City Council's archive (LA/7) at the Public Record Office of Northern Ireland. This archive is a treasure trove for those interested in Belfast, and in the wider fields of urban governance, town planning and municipal politics. In addition, it contains details of the building's history which are beyond the scope of this book to include.

Index

(Note: page numbers in italics refer to illustrations and captions)

BELFAST CITY HALL CENTENARY

First published in 2006 by
Blackstaff Press Limited
4c Heron Wharf, Sydenham Business Park
Belfast BT3 9LE
and Belfast City Council
City Hall, Belfast, BT1 5GS

Design by Dunbar Design, Holywood, County Down
Printed by W. & G. Baird Ltd, County Antrim
A CIP catalogue record for this book is available from
the British Library
ISBN 0-85640-769-0

www.blackstaffpress.com

ACKNOWLEDGEMENTS

I would like to thank the following: the Deputy Keeper of the Public Record Office of Northern Ireland (PRONI), Belfast City Council, BBC Northern Ireland, the Ulster Museum (MAGNI), the Linen Hall Library, Queen's University Library, the Natural History Museum (London), the Getty Archive, the *Irish Times*, the *Belfast Telegraph*, Greenwich Council, Manchester City Council, Stockport Metropolitan Borough Council, the City of Ottawa, Durban City Hall, the National Photographic Archive (Dublin), Scenic Ireland (chrishill@scenicireland.com), Pacemaker Press International, the National Portrait Gallery (London), Rodney Miller Associates, Leslie Stannage Design, the Royal Institute of British Architects. David Cartmill acted as the vital link with Belfast City Council, and I am grateful for his encouragement throughout. I am also grateful for the help of those individuals who gave generously of their time and expertise: Andy White, Ken Patterson, Fionnuala Carson Williams, Patricia McClean, Vivienne Pollock, Paul Carson, Walter Macauley, Keith Jeffery, Seth Linder. The professional support of Patsy Horton, Rachel McNicholl, Janice Smith and Wilma Haire of Blackstaff Press was much appreciated, as was the expert guidance of editor Hilary Bell and proof-reader Anne Tannahill. The picture research for this book was one of the most interesting jobs I have had, but such an image-heavy book demands skills beyond my own capabilities; happily, no design issue is beyond the gifts of Wendy Dunbar. Robert Corbett, the records manager of Belfast City Council, and Ian Montgomery of PRONI gave generously of their knowledge, and their informative personal tour of the City Hall was invaluable. A project of this sort naturally incurs many other debts along the way. My friends and colleagues in the Institute of Irish Studies, Queen's University, Belfast, provided me with a stimulating and supportive environment to work in. Expansive conversations with Drs Dominic Bryan, Kasey Cordell, Oona Frawley, Gordon Gillespie, Neil Fleming and Eamonn Hughes helped me to find my way through this book. At an early stage (and as usual) Professor Alvin Jackson provided me with astute advice. My friend and nineteenth-century expert Dr Maura Cronin made sure I didn't stray too far from the right path. My greatest debts remain to the late Professor Martin Lynn and to Dr Tom Clyde. Martin Lynn encouraged me to undertake this project, and over many coffees helped me to talk through some of its early issues. His friendship and support were very important and are sadly missed. Finally, Dr Tom Clyde provided domestic and editorial support, advice on a range of eclectic subjects, and enthusiasm and patient empathy with the author's anorak tendencies (which happily he shares). This book would have been possible without Tom and our son Hugh but would have been far less enjoyable to do.